potatoes
100 everyday recipes

First published in 2011
LOVE FOOD is an imprint of Parragon Books Ltd

Parragon
Chartist House
15-17 Trim Street
Bath BA1 1HA, UK
www.parragon.com

ISBN: 978-1-4454-3044-7

Printed in China

Produced by Ivy Contract
Photography by Charlie Paul

Notes for the Reader

This book uses both metric and imperial measurements. Follow the same units of measurement throughout; do not mix metric and imperial. All spoon measurements are level: teaspoons are assumed to be 5 ml, and tablespoons are assumed to be 15 ml. Unless otherwise stated, milk is assumed to be full fat, eggs and individual vegetables, such as potatoes, are medium, and pepper is freshly ground black pepper.

The times given are an approximate guide only. Preparation times differ according to the techniques used by different people and the cooking times may also vary from those given. Optional ingredients, variations or serving suggestions have not been included in the calculations.

Recipes using raw or very lightly cooked eggs should be avoided by infants, the elderly, pregnant women, convalescents and anyone suffering from an illness. Pregnant and breastfeeding women are advised to avoid eating peanuts and peanut products. Sufferers from nut allergies should be aware that some of the ready-made ingredients used in the recipes in this book may contain nuts. Always check the packaging before use.

potatoes

introduction

The potato is without doubt one of the most versatile ingredients to have in store. As a nutritional package, potatoes are excellent, containing useful amounts of fibre, minerals such as potassium, and vitamins C and B-complex. Add to this the fact that the scope for making delicious recipes with potatoes as a base is almost unlimited and it will come as no surprise to learn that the potato is one of the world's most popular vegetables, cultivated in almost every country.

Potatoes come in a number of varieties, which lend themselves to different purposes. Potatoes with a 'waxy' texture are suitable for serving boiled – simply place them in a pan, pour in enough boiling water to cover, put on a lid and boil gently until tender. 'Floury' varieties are ideal for mashing or creaming with butter, seasoning and a little hot milk, while both waxy and floury varieties can be roasted in oil in the oven until crisp and golden brown. Most varieties can be baked in their skins, which is the best way

to preserve their nutritional value – in fact, it is always best to cook potatoes in their skins, then if required, peel them when they are cool enough to handle.

When choosing potatoes, make sure they are firm and well-shaped with a smooth, tight skin. New potatoes should be eaten as fresh as possible – they have a wonderful taste, which is greatly enhanced if you melt butter generously over them – but old potatoes can be stored in a cool, dark place. It is important to keep them away from light, as exposure makes them turn green, resulting in an unpleasant flavour as well as an increase in the level of naturally occurring toxins, glycoalkaloids.

This book contains a selection of the very best potato recipes from around the world to inspire you to make the most of this humble vegetable.

soups

leek & potato soup

ingredients

serves 4–6

55 g/2 oz butter
1 onion, chopped
3 leeks, sliced
225 g/8 oz potatoes, peeled and
    cut into 2-cm/³⁄₄-inch cubes
850 ml/1½ pints vegetable stock
salt and pepper
150 ml/5 fl oz single cream
    (optional)
2 tbsp snipped fresh chives,
    to garnish

method

1 Melt the butter in a large pan over medium heat, add the prepared vegetables, and sauté gently for 2–3 minutes until soft but not brown. Pour in the stock, bring to the boil, then reduce the heat and simmer, covered, for 15 minutes.

2 Remove from the heat and blend the soup using a stick blender or food processor.

3 Reheat the soup, season with salt and pepper to taste, and serve in warm bowls, swirled with the cream, if using, and garnished with chives.

potato & vegetable soup with pesto

ingredients

serves 6

2 young carrots
450 g/1 lb potatoes
200 g/7 oz fresh peas in the pods
200 g/7 oz French beans
150 g/5½ oz young courgettes
2 tbsp olive oil
1 garlic clove, crushed
1 large onion, finely chopped
2.5 litres/4½ pints vegetable stock
1 bouquet garni of 2 fresh parsley
    sprigs and 1 bay leaf tied in a
    7.5-cm/3-inch piece of celery
85 g/3 oz dried small soup pasta
1 large tomato, skinned, deseeded
    and chopped or diced
Parmesan cheese shavings,
    to serve

pesto sauce

75 g/2¾ oz fresh basil leaves
1 garlic clove
5 tbsp fruity extra virgin olive oil
salt and pepper

method

1 To make the pesto sauce, put the basil leaves, garlic and olive oil in a food processor and process until well blended. Season with salt and pepper to taste. Transfer to a bowl, then cover and chill until required.

2 Peel the carrots and cut them in half lengthways, then slice. Peel the potatoes and cut into quarters lengthways, then slice. Set aside.

3 Shell the peas. Top and tail the beans and cut them into 2.5-cm/1-inch pieces. Cut the courgette in half lengthways, then slice.

4 Heat the oil in a large saucepan. Add the garlic and cook for 2 minutes, stirring. Add the onion and continue cooking for 2 minutes, until soft. Add the carrots and potatoes and stir for about 30 seconds.

5 Pour in the stock and bring to the boil. Lower the heat, then partially cover and simmer for 8 minutes, until the vegetables are starting to become tender.

6 Stir in the peas, beans, courgette, bouquet garni, pasta and tomato. Season and cook for about 8–10 minutes, or until tender. Discard the bouquet garni. Stir in the pesto sauce, then serve with Parmesan cheese.

sweet potato & stilton soup

ingredients

serves 4

4 tbsp butter
1 large onion, chopped
2 leeks, trimmed and sliced
175 g/6 oz sweet potatoes,
     peeled and diced
850 ml/1½ pints vegetable stock
1 tbsp chopped fresh parsley
1 bay leaf
150 ml/5 fl oz double cream
150 g/5½ oz Stilton cheese,
     crumbled
pepper
2 tbsp finely crumbled Stilton
     cheese, to garnish
thick slices of fresh bread,
     to serve

method

1 Melt the butter in a large saucepan over medium heat. Add the onion and leeks and cook, stirring, for about 3 minutes, until slightly softened. Add the sweet potatoes and cook for another 5 minutes, stirring, then pour in the stock, add the parsley and the bay leaf, and season with pepper. Bring to the boil, then lower the heat, cover the pan, and simmer for about 30 minutes. Remove the soup from the heat and let cool for 10 minutes. Remove and discard the bay leaf.

2 Transfer half of the soup into a food processor and blend until smooth. Return to the pan with the rest of the soup, stir in the cream, and cook for another 5 minutes. Gradually stir in the crumbled Stilton until melted (do not let the soup boil).

3 Remove from the heat and ladle into serving bowls. Garnish with finely crumbled Stilton and serve with slices of fresh bread.

sweet potato & squash soup

ingredients

serves 6

350 g/12 oz sweet potatoes
1 acorn squash
4 shallots
olive oil, for brushing
5–6 garlic cloves, unpeeled
850 ml/1½ pints chicken stock
125 ml/4 fl oz single cream
salt and pepper
chopped fresh chives, to garnish

method

1 Cut the sweet potato, squash, and shallots in half lengthways. Brush the cut sides with oil.

2 Put the vegetables, cut sides down, in a shallow roasting pan. Add the garlic cloves. Roast in a preheated oven, 190°C/375°F/Gas Mark 5, for about 40 minutes, until tender and light brown. Remove the pan from the oven and set aside to cool.

3 When cool, scoop the flesh from the potato and squash halves, and put in a saucepan with the shallots. Squeeze out the soft insides from the garlic and add to the other vegetables.

4 Add the stock and a pinch of salt. Bring just to the boil, then reduce the heat and simmer the soup, partially covered, for about 30 minutes, stirring occasionally, until the vegetables are very tender.

5 Let the soup cool slightly, then process until smooth, in batches if necessary, in a blender or food processor. Return the soup to the pan and stir in most of the cream. Season, then let simmer for 5–10 minutes, until heated through. Serve garnished with chopped fresh chives and a swirl of the remaining cream.

sweet potato & apple soup

ingredients

serves 6

1 tbsp butter

3 leeks, sliced thinly

1 large carrot, sliced thinly

600 g/1 lb 5 oz sweet potatoes,
    peeled and diced

2 large tart eating apples,
    peeled and diced

1.2 litres/2 pints water

freshly grated nutmeg

225 ml/8 fl oz apple juice

225 ml/8 fl oz single cream

salt and pepper

chopped fresh chives or coriander,
    to garnish

method

1 Melt the butter in a large saucepan over low-medium heat. Add the leeks, then cover and cook, stirring frequently, for 6–8 minutes, or until softened but not coloured.

2 Add the carrot, sweet potatoes, apples, and water. Season lightly with salt, pepper, and nutmeg. Bring to the boil, then reduce the heat, cover and simmer, stirring occasionally, for about 20 minutes, until the vegetables are very tender.

3 Let the soup cool slightly, then transfer to a blender or food processor, and process until smooth, working in batches if necessary.

4 Return the soup to the pan and stir in the apple juice. Place over low heat and simmer for about 10 minutes, until heated through.

5 Stir in most of the cream and continue simmering for about 5 minutes, stirring frequently, until heated through. Taste and adjust the seasoning, adding more salt, pepper, and nutmeg, if necessary. Ladle the soup into warm bowls, then garnish with a swirl of the remaining cream, sprinkle with chopped fresh chives or coriander, and serve.

golden pepper & sweet potato soup

ingredients

serves 4

50 g/1¾ oz leek (white part only)
50 g/1¾ oz celery
90 g/3¼ oz potato, peeled
180 g/6¼ oz sweet potato, peeled
75 g/2¾ oz onion, finely chopped
2 garlic cloves, peeled and
　　finely sliced
pinch of ground turmeric
pinch of ground mace
2 bay leaves
850 ml/1½ pints vegetable stock
90 g/3¼ oz deseeded yellow
　　pepper, roasted, skinned
　　and chopped
1 tbsp sugar
2 tsp lemon juice
flat bread, to serve

for the garnish

1 tsp vegetable oil
40 g/1½ oz cooked sweetcorn
　　kernels
½ tsp habanero chilli pepper sauce

method

1 Cut the leek, celery, potato, and sweet potato into ½-inch/1-cm pieces. Put the onion, garlic, leek, and celery into a large, lidded saucepan over a high heat and cook, stirring constantly, for 5 minutes, or until softened but not coloured.

2 Add the potato, sweet potato, turmeric, mace, bay leaves, and stock, stir well and bring to the boil. Reduce the heat, cover, and let simmer for 20 minutes, or until all the vegetables are soft.

3 Meanwhile, in a separate saucepan, heat the oil, add the corn kernels, and stir-fry until golden brown. Remove from the heat and stir in the chilli sauce. Reserve for garnishing the soup.

4 Remove the bay leaves from the soup and discard. Stir in the roasted pepper, sugar and lemon juice. Using a hand-held electric blender or a food processor, blend the soup until smooth.

5 Ladle into warmed soup bowls, sprinkle with the sweetcorn kernel garnish, and serve with flat bread to accompany.

broccoli & cheese soup

ingredients

serves 6

25 g/1 oz butter
1 onion, chopped
2 tsp chopped fresh tarragon,
    plus extra to garnish
450 g/1 lb potatoes, peeled
    and grated
1.7 litres/3 pints vegetable stock
700 g/1 lb 9 oz broccoli,
    cut into small florets
175 g/6 oz Cheddar cheese
1 tbsp chopped fresh parsley
salt and pepper

method

1 Melt the butter in a large, heavy-based saucepan. Add the onion and cook, stirring occasionally, for 5 minutes, until soft. Add the freshly chopped tarragon to the saucepan with the potatoes, season to taste and mix well. Pour in just enough of the stock to cover and bring to the boil. Reduce the heat, cover and simmer for 10 minutes.

2 Meanwhile, bring the remaining stock to the boil in another saucepan. Add the broccoli and cook for 6–8 minutes, until just tender.

3 Remove both pans from the heat, leave to cool slightly then ladle the contents of both into a blender or food processor. Process until smooth, then pour the mixture into a clean saucepan. Grate the cheese, stir into the pan with the parsley and heat gently to warm through but do not allow the soup to boil. Ladle into warmed soup bowls, garnish with tarragon if wished, and serve immediately.

roasted garlic & potato soup

ingredients

serves 4

1 large garlic bulb with large cloves, peeled (about 100 g/ 3½ oz)

2 tsp olive oil, plus extra for brushing

2 large leeks, thinly sliced

1 large onion, finely chopped

500 g/1 lb 2 oz potatoes, diced

1.2 litres/2 pints chicken or vegetable stock

1 bay leaf

150 ml/5 fl oz single cream

freshly grated nutmeg

fresh lemon juice (optional)

salt and pepper

snipped fresh chives and a sprinkle of paprika, to garnish

method

1 Put the garlic cloves in an ovenproof dish, lightly brush with oil and bake in a preheated oven, 180°C/350°F/Gas Mark 4, for about 20 minutes, until golden.

2 Heat the oil in a large saucepan over a medium heat. Add the leeks and onion, cover and cook for about 3 minutes, stirring frequently, until they begin to soften. Add the potatoes, roasted garlic, stock and bay leaf. Season with salt (unless the stock is salty already) and pepper. Bring to the boil, reduce the heat, cover and cook gently for about 30 minutes, until the vegetables are tender.

3 Remove the bay leaf. Allow the soup to cool slightly, then transfer to a blender or food processor and process until smooth, working in batches if necessary. (If using a food processor, strain off the cooking liquid and reserve. Process the soup solids with enough cooking liquid to moisten them, then combine with the remaining liquid.) Return the soup to the saucepan and stir in half the cream and a generous grating of nutmeg. Taste and adjust the seasoning, if necessary, adding a few drops of lemon juice, if using.

4 Reheat over a low heat. Ladle into warmed soup bowls, swirl in remaining cream, garnish with chives and paprika and serve.

carrot & cumin soup

ingredients

serves 4–6

3 tbsp butter or margarine
1 large onion, chopped
1–2 garlic cloves, crushed
350 g/12 oz carrots, sliced
850 ml/1½ pints chicken
  or vegetable stock
¾ tsp ground cumin
2 celery stalks, thinly sliced
115 g/4 oz potato, diced
2 tsp tomato purée
2 tsp lemon juice
2 fresh or dried bay leaves
300 ml/10 fl oz skimmed milk
salt and pepper
celery leaves, to garnish

method

1 Melt the butter or margarine in a large saucepan.
  Add the onion and garlic and cook very gently until
  softened but not coloured.

2 Add the carrots and cook over low heat for 5 minutes
  more, stirring frequently and taking care they do
  not brown.

3 Add the stock, cumin, seasoning, celery, potato, tomato
  purée, lemon juice and bay leaves and bring to the
  boil. Cover and simmer for about 30 minutes, until all
  the vegetables are tender.

4 Remove and discard the bay leaves, cool the soup a
  little, and then press it through a sieve, or process in
  a food processor or blender until smooth.

5 Pour the soup into a clean saucepan, add the milk, and
  bring to the boil over low heat. Taste and adjust the
  seasoning if necessary.

6 Ladle into warmed bowls, garnish each serving with
  a small celery leaf, and serve.

minestrone

ingredients

serves 6

2 fresh basil sprigs
2 fresh marjoram sprigs
2 fresh thyme sprigs
2 tbsp olive oil
2 onions, chopped
2 garlic cloves, chopped
4 tomatoes, peeled and chopped
125 ml/4 fl oz red wine
1.7 litres/3 pints vegetable stock
115 g/4 oz cannellini beans,
    soaked overnight in cold water,
    then drained
2 carrots, chopped
2 potatoes, chopped
1 small turnip, chopped
1 celery stalk, chopped
¼ small cabbage, shredded
55 g/2 oz dried stellette or other
    soup pasta shapes
salt and pepper
2 tbsp freshly grated Parmesan
    cheese, plus extra for serving

method

1 Chop enough fresh basil, marjoram and thyme to fill 2 tablespoons and reserve until required. Heat the olive oil in a heavy-based saucepan. Add the onions and cook, stirring occasionally, for 5 minutes or until softened. Stir in the garlic and cook for an additional 3 minutes, then stir in the chopped tomatoes and the reserved herbs.

2 Add the wine, simmer for 1–2 minutes, then add the stock and drained beans. Bring to the boil, then reduce the heat, partially cover and simmer for 1½ hours.

3 Add the carrots, potatoes and turnip, then cover and simmer for 15 minutes. Add the celery, cabbage and pasta, then cover and simmer for an additional 10 minutes. Season to taste with salt and pepper and stir in the Parmesan cheese. Ladle into warmed bowls and serve with extra Parmesan cheese.

watercress soup

ingredients

serves 4

2 bunches of watercress
  (approx 200 g/7 oz),
  thoroughly cleaned
3 tbsp butter
2 onions, chopped
225 g/8 oz potatoes, peeled
  and roughly chopped
1.2 litres/2 pints vegetable stock
  or water
whole nutmeg, for grating
salt and pepper
125 ml/4 fl oz crème fraîche,
  yogurt, or sour cream

method

1 Remove the leaves from the watercress stalks and set aside. Coarsely chop the stalks.

2 Melt the butter in a large saucepan over medium heat, add the onion and cook for 4–5 minutes until soft. Do not brown.

3 Add the potato to the pan and mix well with the onion. Add the watercress stalks and the stock. Bring to the boil, then reduce the heat, cover, and simmer for 15–20 minutes until the potato is soft.

4 Add the watercress leaves and stir in to heat through. Remove from the heat and use a hand-held stick blender to process the soup until smooth. Alternatively, pour the soup into a blender, process until smooth, and return to the rinsed-out pan. Reheat and season with salt and pepper to taste, adding a good grating of nutmeg, if using.

5 Serve in warm bowls with the crème fraîche spooned on top.

chicken & potato soup with bacon

ingredients

serves 4

1 tbsp butter
2 garlic cloves, chopped
1 onion, sliced
250 g/9 oz smoked lean bacon, chopped
2 large leeks, trimmed and sliced
2 tbsp plain flour
1 litre/1¾ pints chicken stock
800 g/1 lb 12 oz potatoes, peeled and chopped
200 g/7 oz skinless chicken breast, chopped
4 tbsp double cream
salt and pepper
grilled bacon, chopped, to garnish
fresh crusty rolls, to serve

method

1 Melt the butter in a large saucepan over medium heat. Add the garlic and onion and cook, stirring, for 3 minutes, until slightly softened. Add the chopped bacon and leeks and cook for another 3 minutes, stirring continuously.

2 In a bowl, mix the flour with enough stock to make a smooth paste and stir it into the pan. Cook, stirring, for 2 minutes. Pour in the remaining stock, then add the potatoes and chicken. Season with salt and pepper. Bring to the boil, then lower the heat and simmer for 25 minutes, until the chicken and potatoes are tender and cooked through.

3 Stir in the cream and cook for 2 minutes more, then remove from the heat and ladle into serving bowls. Garnish the soup with chopped bacon and serve with fresh crusty rolls.

sausage & red cabbage soup

ingredients

serves 4

2 tbsp olive oil
1 garlic clove, chopped
1 large onion, chopped
1 large leek, sliced
2 tbsp cornflour
1 litre/1¾ pints vegetable stock
450 g/1 lb potatoes, sliced
200 g/7 oz skinless sausages, sliced
150 g/5 oz red cabbage, chopped
200 g/7 oz canned black-eyed beans, drained
125 ml/4 fl oz double cream
salt and pepper
ground paprika, to garnish

method

1 Heat the oil in a large saucepan. Add the garlic and onion and cook over a medium heat, stirring, for 3 minutes, until slightly softened. Add the leek and cook for a further 3 minutes, stirring.

2 In a bowl, mix the cornflour with enough stock to make a smooth paste, then stir it into the pan. Cook, stirring, for 2 minutes. Stir in the remaining stock, then add the potatoes and sausages. Season with salt and pepper. Bring to the boil, then lower the heat and simmer for 25 minutes.

3 Add the red cabbage and beans and cook for 10 minutes, then stir in the cream and cook for a further 5 minutes. Remove from the heat and ladle into serving bowls. Garnish with ground paprika and serve immediately.

breton fish soup with cider & sorrel

ingredients

serves 4

2 tsp butter
1 large leek, thinly sliced
2 shallots, finely chopped
125 ml/4 fl oz dry cider
300 ml/10 fl oz fish stock
250 g/9 oz potatoes, diced
1 bay leaf
4 tbsp plain flour
200 ml/7 fl oz milk
200 ml/7 fl oz double cream
55 g/2 oz sorrel leaves
350 g/12 oz skinless monkfish fish
    or cod fillets, cut into
    2.5-cm/1-inch pieces
salt and pepper

method

1 Melt the butter in a large saucepan over low-medium heat. Add the leek and shallots, and cook, stirring frequently, for 5 minutes or until they start to soften. Add the cider and bring to the boil.

2 Stir in the stock, potatoes and bay leaf with a large pinch of salt (unless the stock is salty) and return to the boil. Reduce the heat, cover, and cook gently for 10 minutes.

3 Put the flour in a small bowl and very slowly whisk in a few tablespoons of the milk to make a thick paste. Stir in a little more milk to make a smooth liquid. Adjust the heat so that the soup bubbles gently. Stir in the flour mixture and cook, stirring frequently, for 5 minutes. Add the remaining milk and half the cream. Cook for an additional 10 minutes or until the potatoes are tender.

4 Finely chop the sorrel and combine with the remaining cream. Stir into the soup and add the fish. Cook, stirring occasionally, for an additional 3 minutes or until the monkfish stiffens or the cod just begins to flake. Taste the soup and adjust the seasoning, if necessary. Ladle into warmed bowls and serve.

haddock & potato soup

ingredients

serves 4

2 tbsp butter
1 onion, chopped
1 leek, chopped
2 tbsp plain flour
850 ml/1½ pints milk
1 bay leaf
2 tbsp chopped fresh parsley,
    plus extra to garnish
350 g/12 oz smoked haddock
    fillets, skinned
450 g/1 lb potatoes, cooked
    and mashed
6 tbsp double cream
salt and pepper
crusty rolls and green salad,
    to serve

method

1 Melt the butter in a large saucepan over medium heat
   add the onion and leek and cook, stirring frequently,
   for 3 minutes, or until slightly softened. Mix the flour
   in a bowl with enough of the milk to make a smooth
   paste, then stir into the pan. Cook, stirring constantly,
   for 2 minutes, then gradually stir in the remaining milk
   Add the bay leaf and parsley and season to taste with
   salt and pepper. Bring to the boil, then reduce the heat
   and simmer for 15 minutes.

2 Rinse the haddock fillets under cold running water,
   drain, then cut into bite-size chunks. Add to the soup
   and cook for 15 minutes, or until the fish is tender and
   cooked right through. Add the mashed potatoes and
   stir in the cream. Cook for a further 2–3 minutes, then
   remove from the heat and remove and discard the
   bay leaf.

3 Ladle into warmed serving bowls, garnish with
   chopped parsley, and serve with crusty rolls and
   a green salad.

quick clam chowder

ingredients

serves 4

2 tsp corn oil
115 g/4 oz rindless lean
    bacon, diced
2 tbsp butter
1 onion, chopped
2 celery stalks, chopped
2 potatoes, chopped
2 leeks, sliced
400 g/14 oz canned chopped
    tomatoes
3 tbsp chopped fresh parsley
1.2 litres/2 pints fish stock
550 g/1 lb 4 oz canned clams,
    drained and rinsed
salt and pepper

method

1 Heat the oil in a heavy-based saucepan. Add the bacon and cook over medium heat, stirring, for 5 minutes or until the fat runs and it begins to crisp. Remove from the pan, drain on kitchen paper and reserve.

2 Melt the butter in the pan. Add the onion, celery and potatoes with a pinch of salt. Cover and cook over low heat, stirring occasionally, for 10 minutes, or until soft.

3 Stir in the leeks, the tomatoes and their juices, and 2 tablespoons of the parsley. Pour in the stock, bring to the boil, reduce the heat and simmer for 10–15 minutes, or until the vegetables are tender. Season to taste with salt and pepper and stir in the clams.

4 Heat the soup gently for 2–3 minutes, then ladle into warmed bowls, garnish with the remaining parsley and reserved bacon, and serve.

salads

potato salad

ingredients

serves 4

700 g/1 lb 9 oz tiny new potatoes
8 spring onions
1 hard-boiled egg (optional)
250 ml/9 fl oz low-fat mayonnaise
1 tsp paprika
salt and pepper
2 tbsp chopped fresh chives
pinch of paprika, to garnish

method

1 Bring a large saucepan of lightly salted water to the boil. Add the potatoes to the pan and cook for about 10–15 minutes, or until they are just tender. Drain the potatoes in a colander and rinse them under cold running water until they are completely cold. Drain them again thoroughly. Transfer the potatoes to a mixing bowl and set aside.

2 Trim and slice the spring onions thinly on the diagonal. Chop the hard-boiled egg, if using.

3 Combine the mayonnaise, paprika and salt and pepper to taste in a bowl until well blended. Pour the mixture over the potatoes. Add the sliced spring onions and chopped egg, if using, and toss together.

4 Transfer the potato salad to a serving bowl. Sprinkle with chopped chives and a pinch of paprika. Cover and chill in the refrigerator until ready to serve.

nests of chinese salad

ingredients

serves 4

potato nests
450 g/1 lb grated floury potatoes
125 g/4½ oz cornflour
vegetable oil, for deep-frying
fresh chives, to garnish

salad
125 g/4½ oz pineapple, diced
1 green pepper, deseeded
    and cut into strips
1 carrot, cut into thin strips
50 g/1¾ oz mangetout,
    thickly sliced
4 baby corn cobs,
    halved lengthways
25 g/1 oz bean sprouts
2 spring onions, sliced

dressing
1 tbsp honey
1 tsp light soy sauce
1 garlic clove, crushed
1 tsp lemon juice

method

1 To make the nests, rinse the potatoes several times in cold water. Drain well on kitchen paper so that they are completely dry. This is to prevent the potatoes from spitting when they are cooked in the oil. Place the potatoes in a large mixing bowl. Add the cornflour, mixing well to coat the potatoes.

2 Half fill a wok with vegetable oil and heat until it is smoking. Line a 15-cm/6-inch diameter wire sieve with a quarter of the potato mixture and press another sieve of the same size on top.

3 Lower the sieves into the oil and cook for 2 minutes, until the potato nest is golden brown and crisp. Remove from the wok, and drain well on kitchen paper. Repeat 3 more times, to use up all of the mixture and make a total of 4 nests. Set aside to cool.

4 Combine all the salad ingredients, then spoon the salad into the potato baskets. Combine the dressing ingredients. Pour the dressing over the salad. Garnish with fresh chives and then serve immediately.

indian potato salad

ingredients

serves 4

900 g/2 lb diced floury potatoes
75 g/2¾ oz small broccoli florets
1 small mango, diced
4 spring onions, sliced
salt and pepper
small cooked spiced poppadoms,
    to serve

dressing

½ tsp ground cumin
½ tsp ground coriander
1 tbsp mango chutney
150 ml/5 fl oz low-fat plain yogurt
1 tsp chopped fresh ginger
2 tbsp chopped fresh coriander

method

1 Cook the potatoes in a large saucepan of boiling water for 10 minutes, or until tender. Drain well and place in a mixing bowl.

2 Meanwhile, blanch the broccoli florets in a separate saucepan of boiling water for 2 minutes. Drain the broccoli well and add to the potatoes in the bowl.

3 When the potatoes and broccoli have cooled, add the diced mango and sliced spring onions. Season to taste with salt and pepper and mix well to combine.

4 In a small bowl, stir the dressing ingredients together. Spoon the dressing over the potato mixture and mix together carefully, taking care not to break up the potatoes and broccoli.

5 Serve the salad immediately, accompanied by the small cooked spiced poppadoms.

herby potato salad

ingredients

serves 4

500 g/1 lb 2 oz new potatoes
16 vine-ripened cherry
    tomatoes, halved
55 g/2 oz black olives, pitted
    and roughly chopped
4 spring onions, finely sliced
2 tbsp chopped fresh mint
2 tbsp chopped fresh parsley
2 tbsp chopped fresh coriander
juice of 1 lemon
3 tbsp extra virgin olive oil
salt and pepper

method

1 Cook the potatoes in a saucepan of lightly salted
    boiling water for 15 minutes, or until tender. Drain, the
    cool slightly before peeling off the skins. Cut into halve
    or quarters, depending on the size of the potato. Then
    combine with the tomatoes, olives, spring onions and
    herbs in a salad bowl.

2 Mix the lemon juice and oil together in a small bowl
    or jug and pour over the potato salad. Season to taste
    with salt and pepper before serving.

grilled new potato salad

ingredients

serves 4

675 g/1 lb 8 oz new
    potatoes, scrubbed
3 tbsp olive oil
2 tbsp chopped fresh thyme
1 tsp paprika
4 smoked bacon rashers
salt and pepper
fresh parsley sprig, to garnish

dressing

4 tbsp mayonnaise
1 tbsp garlic wine vinegar
2 garlic cloves, crushed
1 tbsp chopped fresh parsley

method

1 Cook the new potatoes in a large saucepan of boiling
    water for about 10 minutes, until tender. Drain well and
    turn into a bowl.

2 Combine the olive oil, chopped thyme and paprika,
    and pour the mixture over the warm potatoes, tossing
    gently to coat.

3 Place the bacon rashers under a preheated medium
    grill and cook, turning once, for 5 minutes, until crisp.
    When cooked, roughly chop the bacon and keep
    warm.

4 Transfer the potatoes to the grill pan and cook for
    10 minutes, turning once.

5 Combine the dressing ingredients in a small serving
    bowl. Transfer the potatoes and bacon to a large
    serving bowl. Season to taste with salt and pepper
    and mix together thoroughly.

6 Spoon over the dressing. Garnish with a parsley sprig
    and serve immediately for a warm salad. Alternatively,
    cool and serve chilled.

sweet potato salad

ingredients

serves 4

500 g/1 lb 2 oz diced sweet
    potatoes
4 tbsp butter
1 tbsp lemon juice
1 garlic clove, crushed
1 red pepper, deseeded
    and diced
1 green pepper, deseeded
    and diced
2 bananas, peeled and thickly
    sliced
2 thick slices white bread,
    crusts removed, diced
salt and pepper

dressing

2 tbsp honey
2 tbsp chopped fresh chives
2 tbsp lemon juice
2 tbsp olive oil

method

1 Cook the sweet potatoes in a large saucepan of boiling
    water for 10–15 minutes, until tender. Drain thoroughly
    and set aside.

2 Meanwhile, melt the butter in a frying pan. Add the
    lemon juice, garlic and peppers and cook, stirring
    constantly, for 3 minutes. Add the bananas and cook
    for 1 minute. Remove the mixture from the pan with
    a slotted spoon and stir into the potatoes.

3 Add the bread cubes to the frying pan and cook,
    stirring frequently, for 2 minutes, until they are golden
    brown on all sides.

4 Mix the dressing ingredients together in a small bowl
    and heat until well combined.

5 Spoon the potato mixture into a serving dish and
    season to taste with salt and pepper. Pour the dressing
    over the potatoes and sprinkle the croûtons over the
    top. Serve the sweet potato salad immediately.

sweet potato salad with green olives

ingredients

serves 4–6

3 tbsp olive or argan oil

1 red or golden onion, roughly chopped

25 g/1 oz fresh ginger, peeled and grated

1 tsp cumin seeds

450 g/1 lb orange sweet potatoes, peeled and cut into bite-sized cubes

½ tsp paprika

8–10 green olives

rind of ½ preserved lemon, finely chopped

juice of ½ lemon

1 small bunch of fresh flat-leaf parsley, finely chopped

1 small bunch of fresh coriander, finely chopped

salt and pepper

method

1 Heat 2 tablespoons of the oil in a tagine or heavy-based, flameproof casserole, add the onion and cook over a medium heat for 2–3 minutes, stirring frequently, until it begins to colour. Add the ginger and cumin seeds and cook for 1–2 minutes, stirring, until fragrant.

2 Toss in the sweet potatoes along with the paprika and the remaining oil. Season to taste with salt and pepper and pour in enough water just to cover the base of the tagine or casserole. Cover and cook gently for 10 minutes, or until the sweet potato is tender but firm and the liquid has reduced.

3 Toss in the olives and preserved lemon rind and refresh with the lemon juice. Serve warm or at room temperature, with the parsley and coriander scattered over the top.

potato, rocket & apple salad

ingredients

serves 4

600 g/1 lb 5 oz potatoes,
    unpeeled and sliced
2 green eating apples,
    cored and diced
1 tsp lemon juice
25 g/1 oz walnut pieces
125 g/4½ oz goat's cheese, diced
150 g/5½ oz rocket leaves
salt and pepper

dressing

2 tbsp olive oil
1 tbsp red wine vinegar
1 tsp honey
1 tsp fennel seeds

method

1 Cook the potatoes in a saucepan of boiling water for
15 minutes, until tender. Drain thoroughly and cool.
Transfer the cooled potatoes to a serving bowl.

2 Toss the diced apples in the lemon juice, then drain,
and stir them into the potatoes. Add the walnut pieces,
cheese cubes, and rocket leaves, then toss the salad to
mix. Season to taste.

3 In a small bowl or jug, whisk the dressing ingredients
together and then pour the dressing over the salad.
Serve immediately.

variation

For a subtler, less peppery taste, replace the rocket with
150 g/5½ oz of baby spinach instead.

radish & cucumber salad

ingredients

serves 4

500 g/1 lb 2 oz new potatoes,
    scrubbed and halved
½ cucumber, sliced thinly
2 tsp salt
1 bunch of radishes,
    thinly sliced

dressing

1 tbsp Dijon mustard
2 tbsp olive oil
1 tbsp white wine vinegar
2 tbsp chopped mixed herbs

method

1 Cook the potatoes in a saucepan of boiling water for 10–15 minutes, or until tender. Drain thoroughly and set aside to cool.

2 Meanwhile, spread out the cucumber slices on a plate and sprinkle with the salt. Set aside for 30 minutes, then rinse well under cold running water, and pat thoroughly dry with kitchen paper.

3 Arrange the cucumber and radish slices on a serving plate in a decorative pattern and pile the cooked potatoes in the centre of the slices.

4 In a small bowl, combine all the dressing ingredients, whisking until thoroughly mixed. Pour the dressing over the salad, tossing well to coat all of the ingredients. Chill in the refrigerator before serving.

italian sausage salad

ingredients

serves 4

450 g/1 lb waxy potatoes
1 radicchio or lollo rosso lettuce
1 green pepper, deseeded
    and sliced
175 g/6 oz Italian sausage, sliced
1 red onion, halved and sliced
125 g/4½ oz sun-dried tomatoes
    in oil, drained and sliced
2 tbsp shredded fresh basil

dressing

1 tbsp balsamic vinegar
1 tsp tomato purée
2 tbsp olive oil
salt and pepper

method

1 Cook the potatoes in a large saucepan of boiling water for about 20 minutes, or until cooked through. Drain and cool.

2 Separate the radicchio leaves or lollo rosso lettuce leaves. Line a large serving platter with the leaves.

3 Slice the cooled potatoes and arrange them in layers on the leaf-lined platter together with the sliced green pepper, sliced Italian sausage, red onion and sun-dried tomatoes. Sprinkle with the shredded fresh basil.

4 In a small bowl, whisk the balsamic vinegar, tomato purée and olive oil together and season to taste with salt and pepper. Pour the dressing over the salad and serve immediately.

tuna, egg & potato salad

ingredients

serves 4

350 g/12 oz new potatoes,
  unpeeled
1 hard-boiled egg,
  cooled and shelled
3 tbsp olive oil
1½ tbsp white wine vinegar
115 g/4 oz canned tuna in oil,
  drained and flaked
2 shallots, finely chopped
1 tomato, peeled and diced
2 tbsp chopped fresh parsley
salt and pepper

method

1 Cook the potatoes in a saucepan of lightly salted boiling water for 10 minutes, then remove from the heat, cover and stand for 15–20 minutes, or until tender. Drain, then peel and thinly slice.

2 Meanwhile, slice the egg, then cut each slice in half. Whisk the olive oil and vinegar together in a bowl and season to taste with salt and pepper. Spoon a little of the vinaigrette into a serving dish to coat the base.

3 Place half the potato slices over the base of the dish and season to taste with salt, then top with half the flaked tuna, half the egg slices and half the shallots. Pour over half the remaining dressing. Make a second layer with the remaining potato slices, tuna, egg and shallots. Pour over the remaining dressing.

4 Finally, top the salad with the tomato and parsley. Cover with clingfilm and stand in a cool place for 1–2 hours before serving.

mackerel & potato salad

ingredients

serves 4

125 g/4½ oz new potatoes, scrubbed and diced
225 g/8 oz mackerel fillets, skinned
1.2 litres/2 pints water
1 bay leaf
1 slice of lemon
1 eating apple, cored and diced
1 shallot, thinly sliced
3 tbsp white wine vinegar
1 tsp sunflower oil
1½ tsp caster sugar
¼ tsp Dijon mustard
salt and pepper

to serve

2 tbsp low-fat plain yogurt
¼ cucumber, thinly sliced
1 bunch of watercress
1 tbsp snipped fresh chives

method

1 Steam the potatoes over a saucepan of simmering water for 10 minutes, or until tender.

2 Meanwhile, cut the mackerel into bite-size pieces. Bring the water to the boil in a large, shallow saucepan, then reduce the heat so that it is just simmering and add the fish pieces, bay leaf and lemon. Poach for 3 minutes, or until the flesh of the fish is opaque. Remove with a slotted spoon and transfer to a serving dish.

3 Drain the potatoes and transfer to a large bowl. Add the apple and shallot and mix well, then spoon the mixture over the fish.

4 Mix the vinegar, oil, sugar and mustard together in a jug, season to taste with salt and pepper, and whisk thoroughly. Pour the dressing over the potato mixture. Cover and chill in the refrigerator for up to 6 hours.

5 To serve, spread the yogurt over the salad, then arrange the cucumber decoratively on top. Add sprigs of watercress and sprinkle with the chives.

spicy chicken salad

ingredients

serves 4

2 skinless, boneless chicken
    breast portions, about
    125 g/4½ oz each
2 tbsp butter
1 fresh red chilli, deseeded
    and chopped
1 tbsp honey
½ tsp ground cumin
2 tbsp chopped fresh coriander
600 g/1 lb 5 oz diced potatoes
50 g/1¾ oz French beans, halved
1 red pepper, deseeded
    and cut into thin strips
2 tomatoes, deseeded and diced

dressing

2 tbsp olive oil
pinch of chilli powder
1 tbsp garlic wine vinegar
pinch of caster sugar
1 tbsp chopped fresh coriander

method

1 Cut the chicken into thin strips. Melt the butter in a
    heavy saucepan and add the chicken strips, fresh red
    chilli, honey and cumin. Cook for 10 minutes, turning
    until cooked through. Transfer the mixture to a bowl
    and cool, then stir in the chopped coriander.

2 Meanwhile, cook the diced potatoes in a saucepan
    of boiling water for 10 minutes, until they are tender.
    Drain and cool.

3 Blanch the French beans in a saucepan of boiling wat
    for 3 minutes. Drain well and leave to cool. Combine
    the French beans and potatoes in a mixing bowl. Add
    the pepper strips and tomatoes to the potato mixtur
    Stir in the chicken mixture.

4 In a small bowl, whisk the dressing ingredients
    together and pour the dressing over the salad, tossing
    well. Transfer the spicy chicken salad to a serving bow
    or large platter and serve immediately.

light meals

potato cakes

ingredients

serves 8–10

550 g/1 lb 4 oz floury potatoes,
    peeled and cut into chunks
salt and pepper
25 g/1 oz butter, plus extra
    to serve
1 egg (optional)
115 g/4 oz plain flour

method

1 To make the mashed potato, cook the potatoes in
    a large saucepan of boiling salted water for 15–20
    minutes. Drain well and mash with a potato masher
    until smooth. Season to taste with salt and pepper
    and add the butter. Mix in the egg, if using.

2 Turn the mixture out into a large mixing bowl and
    add enough of the flour to make a light dough.
    Work quickly as you do not want the potato to cool
    too much.

3 Place the dough on a lightly floured work surface
    and roll out carefully to a thickness of 5 mm/¼ inch.
    Using a 6-cm/2½-inch pastry cutter, cut the dough
    into circles.

4 Heat a greased frying pan. Cook the potato cakes in
    batches for 4–5 minutes on each side until they are
    golden brown.

5 Keep warm on a hot plate and serve at once with lots
    of fresh butter.

feta & potato cakes

ingredients

serves 4

500 g/1 lb 2 oz floury
    potatoes, unpeeled
4 spring onions, chopped
115 g/4 oz Feta cheese, crumbled
2 tsp chopped fresh thyme
1 egg, beaten
1 tbsp lemon juice
plain flour, for dusting
3 tbsp corn oil
salt and pepper
fresh chives, to garnish

method

1 Cook the potatoes in lightly salted boiling water for
about 25 minutes, or until tender. Drain and peel.
Place the potatoes in a bowl and mash well with a
potato masher or fork.

2 Add the spring onions, Feta, thyme, egg and lemon
juice and season to taste with salt and pepper. Mix
thoroughly. Cover the bowl with clingfilm and chill
in the refrigerator for 1 hour.

3 Take small handfuls of the potato mixture and roll into
balls about the size of a walnut between the palms of
your hands. Flatten each one slightly and dust all over
with flour. Heat the oil in a frying pan over high heat
and cook the potato cakes, in batches if necessary, until
golden brown on both sides. Drain on kitchen paper
and serve, garnished with the fresh chives.

potato, leek & feta patties

ingredients

serves 4

1 whole garlic bulb
115 g/4 oz sweet potatoes,
    peeled and cut into chunks
175 g/6 oz carrots, peeled
    and chopped
115 g/4 oz leeks, trimmed
    and finely chopped
55 g/2 oz Feta cheese, crumbled
1–2 tsp Tabasco sauce,
    or to taste
1 tbsp chopped fresh coriander
pepper
fresh herbs or salad,
    to garnish
tomato ketchup, to serve
    (optional)

method

1 Break the garlic bulb open, place in a small roasting tin and roast in a preheated oven, 190°C/375°F/Gas Mark 5, for 20 minutes, or until soft. Remove and when cool enough to handle, squeeze out the roasted garlic flesh.

2 Cook the sweet potatoes and carrots in a large saucepan of boiling water for 15 minutes, or until soft. Drain and mash then mix in the roasted garlic flesh.

3 Add the leeks, Feta cheese, Tabasco sauce, coriander and pepper to the sweet potato mixture. Cover and leave to chill in the refrigerator for at least 30 minutes.

4 Using slightly dampened hands, shape the sweet potato mixture into 8 small round patties and place on a non-stick baking sheet. Bake for 15–20 minutes, or until piping hot. Garnish with fresh herbs or salad and serve with tomato ketchup, if using.

tomato & potato tortilla

ingredients

serves 6

1 kg/2 lb 4 oz potatoes, peeled
    and cut into small cubes
2 tbsp olive oil
1 bunch spring onions, chopped
115 g/4 oz cherry tomatoes
6 eggs
3 tbsp water
2 tbsp chopped fresh parsley
salt and pepper

method

1 Cook the potatoes in a saucepan of lightly salted boiling water for 8–10 minutes, or until tender. Drain and reserve until required.

2 Preheat the grill to medium. Heat the oil in a large frying pan. Add the spring onions and fry until just soft. Add the potatoes and fry for 3–4 minutes, until coated with oil and hot. Smooth the top and scatter over the tomatoes.

3 Mix the eggs, water, salt and pepper and parsley together in a bowl, then pour into the frying pan. Cook over a very gentle heat for 10–15 minutes, until the tortilla looks fairly set.

4 Place the frying pan under the hot grill and cook until the top is brown and set. Leave to cool for 10–15 minutes before sliding out of the frying pan on to a chopping board. Cut into wedges and serve immediately.

open rösti omelette

ingredients

serves 4

55 g/2 oz old potatoes,
  peeled and grated
1 onion, grated
2 garlic cloves, crushed
1 carrot, about 115 g/4 oz,
  peeled and grated
4 sprays olive oil
1 yellow pepper, peeled
  and thinly sliced
1 courgette, about 85 g/3 oz,
  trimmed and thinly sliced
85 g/3 oz cherry tomatoes,
  halved
2 eggs
3 egg whites
1 tbsp snipped fresh chives
pepper
fresh rocket, to garnish

method

1 Put the grated potatoes into a large bowl and cover with cold water. Leave for 15 minutes then drain, rinse thoroughly and dry on absorbent kitchen paper or a clean tea towel. Mix with the grated onion, garlic and carrot.

2 Heat a heavy-based non-stick frying pan and spray with the oil. Add the potato, onion, garlic and carrot mixture and cook over a low heat for 5 minutes, pressing the vegetables down firmly with a spatula. Add the peeled pepper and courgette slices. Cover with a lid or crumpled piece of foil and cook very gently, stirring occasionally, for 5 minutes.

3 Add the halved cherry tomatoes and cook for a further 2 minutes, or until the vegetables are tender.

4 Beat the whole eggs, egg whites, pepper to taste and the chives together in a bowl. Pour over the vegetable mixture and cook for 4–5 minutes, stirring the egg from the sides of the pan towards the centre, until the vegetables are tender and the eggs are set. Serve immediately, garnished with rocket leaves

potato fritters with onion & tomato relish

ingredients

serves 8

55 g/2 oz wholemeal flour
½ tsp ground coriander
½ tsp cumin seeds
¼ tsp chilli powder
½ tsp turmeric
¼ tsp salt
1 egg
3 tbsp milk
350 g/12 oz potatoes, peeled
1–2 garlic cloves, crushed
4 spring onions, chopped
55 g/2 oz sweetcorn kernels
vegetable oil, for shallow
    frying

onion & tomato relish

1 onion, peeled
225 g/8 oz tomatoes
2 tbsp chopped fresh coriander
2 tbsp chopped fresh mint
2 tbsp lemon juice
½ tsp roasted cumin seeds
¼ tsp salt
pinch of cayenne pepper

method

1 First make the relish. Dice the onion and tomatoes and place in a bowl with the remaining ingredients. Mix together well and leave to stand for at least 15 minutes before serving to allow the flavours to blend.

2 Place the flour in a bowl, stir in the spices and salt and make a well in the centre. Add the egg and milk and mix to form a fairly thick batter. Coarsely grate the potatoes, place them in a sieve and rinse well under cold running water. Drain and squeeze them dry, then stir into the batter with the garlic, spring onions and sweetcorn and mix to combine thoroughly.

3 Heat a little vegetable oil in a large frying pan and add a few tablespoons of the mixture at a time, flattening each one to form a thin cake. Fry over a low heat, turning frequently, for 2–3 minutes, or until golden brown and cooked through. Drain the fritters on kitchen paper and keep them hot while frying the remaining mixture. Serve the fritters hot with the relish.

variation

For a delicious alternative, replace the onion and tomato relish with aïoli (see page 116).

feta & spinach omelette

ingredients

serves 4

6 tbsp butter
1.3 kg/3 lb diced
      waxy potatoes
3 garlic cloves, crushed
1 tsp paprika
2 tomatoes, skinned,
      deseeded, and diced
12 eggs
pepper

filling

225 g/8 oz baby spinach
1 tsp fennel seeds
125 g/4¹/₂ oz Feta cheese, diced
4 tbsp plain yogurt

method

1 Heat 2 tablespoons of the butter in a frying pan and cook the potatoes over low heat, stirring constantly, for 7–10 minutes, until golden. Transfer to a bowl.

2 Add the garlic, paprika and tomatoes to the frying pa and cook for 2 minutes.

3 Whisk the eggs together and season with pepper. Pour the eggs into the potatoes and mix well.

4 Cook the spinach for 1 minute in boiling water, until just wilted. Drain and refresh under cold running wa Pat dry with kitchen paper. Stir in the fennel seeds, F cheese and yogurt.

5 Heat a quarter of the remaining butter in a 15-cm/ 6-inch omelette pan. Ladle a quarter of the egg and potato mixture into the pan. Cook, turning once, for 2 minutes, until set.

6 Transfer the omelette to a serving plate. Spoon a quarter of the spinach mixture onto one half of the omelette, fold the omelette in half over the filling. Repeat to make a further 3 omelettes, then serve.

sweet potato blinis

ingredients

serves 4

115 g/4 oz sweet potatoes,
   peeled and cut into chunks
1 tsp ground allspice
55 g/2 oz wholewheat flour
1 egg
150 ml/5 fl oz skimmed milk
1 egg white
pepper

filling

85 g/3 oz prosciutto, fat discarded
3 tomatoes, thickly sliced
115 g/4 oz cream cheese
1 tbsp finely grated lemon rind
1 tbsp chopped fresh parsley
25 g/1 oz rocket leaves

method

1 Cook the sweet potatoes in boiling water over medium heat for 15 minutes, or until soft. Drain and mash until smooth, then season with pepper to taste and stir in the ground allspice and flour. Place in a mixing bowl.

2 Add the whole egg and beat it into the mashed sweet potatoes, then gradually stir in the milk to give a thick batter consistency. Set aside until required.

3 To prepare the filling, first preheat the grill. Cut the prosciutto into strips. Place the tomatoes on a foil-lined grill rack and, just before serving, cook under the preheated hot grill for 3–4 minutes or until hot. Blend the cream cheese with the lemon rind and parsley. Set aside.

4 Whisk the egg white until stiff and stir it into the sweet potato batter. Heat a non-stick frying pan until hot, then place 3–4 spoonfuls of the batter in the frying pan and swirl to form a 7.5-cm/3-inch circle. Cook for 2–3 minutes, or until set, then turn over and cook for a further 2–3 minutes, or until golden. Keep warm while you cook the remaining batter.

5 Place 2–3 blinis on a plate and top with a little rocket, prosciutto and grilled tomato slices, then spoon over a little of the cream cheese and serve.

bubble & squeak

ingredients

serves 2–3

450 g/1 lb green cabbage
1 onion, thinly sliced
4 tbsp olive oil
salt and pepper

mashed potato

450 g/1 lb floury potatoes,
    such as King Edwards,
    Maris Piper or Desirée,
    peeled and cut into chunks
55 g/2 oz butter
3 tbsp hot milk
salt and pepper

method

1 To make the mashed potato, cook the potatoes in a large saucepan of boiling salted water for 15–20 minutes. Drain well and mash with a potato masher until smooth. Season with salt and pepper, add the butter and milk and stir well.

2 Cut the cabbage into quarters, remove the centre sta and shred finely. In a large frying pan, fry the onion in half the oil until soft.

3 Add the cabbage to the pan and stir-fry for 2–3 minutes until softened. Season with salt and pepper, add the mashed potato and mix together well. Press the mixture firmly into the frying pan and allow to cook over a high heat for 4–5 minutes so that the bas is crispy. Place a plate over the frying pan and invert the pan so that the potato cake falls onto the plate.

4 Add the remaining oil to the pan, reheat and slip the cake back into the pan with the uncooked side down Continue to cook for a further 5 minutes until the bottom is crispy. Turn out onto a hot plate and cut int wedges for serving. Serve immediately.

rösti with roasted vegetables

ingredients

serves 4

900 g/2 lb potatoes,
    halved if large
corn oil, for cooking
salt and pepper

roasted vegetables

2 tbsp extra virgin olive oil
1 tbsp balsamic vinegar
1 tsp honey
1 red pepper, deseeded
    and quartered
2 courgettes, sliced lengthways
2 red onions, quartered
1 small fennel bulb,
    cut into thin wedges
16 vine-ripened tomatoes
8 garlic cloves
2 fresh rosemary sprigs

pesto dressing

2 tbsp pesto
1 tbsp boiling water
1 tbsp extra virgin olive oil

method

1 For the roasted vegetables, mix together the oil,
   vinegar and honey in a large, shallow dish. Add the
   red pepper, courgettes, onions, fennel, tomatoes, garlic
   and rosemary and toss in the marinade. Marinate for
   1 hour.

2 Cook the potatoes in a saucepan of lightly salted
   boiling water for 8–10 minutes, or until partially
   cooked. Cool, then coarsely grate.

3 Transfer the vegetables, except the tomatoes and
   garlic, and the marinade to a roasting tin. Roast in
   a preheated oven, 200°C/400°F/Gas Mark 6, for
   25 minutes, then add the tomatoes and garlic and
   roast for a further 15 minutes, or until the vegetables
   are tender and slightly blackened around the edges.

4 Meanwhile, cook the rösti. Take a quarter of the potato
   mixture in your hands and form into a roughly shaped
   cake. Heat just enough oil to cover the bottom of
   a frying pan over medium heat. Put the cakes, 2 at a
   time, into the frying pan and flatten with a spatula to
   form circles about 2 cm/³⁄₄ inch thick.

5 Cook the rösti for 6 minutes on each side, or until
   golden brown and crisp. Mix the dressing ingredients.
   To serve, top each rösti with the roasted vegetables
   and drizzle with a little pesto dressing. Season to taste.

potato ravioli

ingredients

serves 4

filling

1 tbsp vegetable oil
125 g/4½ oz minced beef
1 shallot, diced
1 garlic clove, crushed
1 tbsp plain flour
1 tbsp tomato purée
150 ml/5 fl oz beef stock
1 celery stalk, chopped
2 tomatoes, skinned and diced
2 tsp chopped fresh basil
salt and pepper

ravioli

450 g/1 lb diced floury potatoes
3 medium egg yolks
3 tbsp olive oil
salt and pepper
175 g/6 oz plain flour, plus
    extra for dusting
5 tbsp butter, for frying
shredded basil leaves, to garnish

method

1 To make the filling, heat the oil in a saucepan and cook the beef for 3–4 minutes, breaking it up with a spoon. Add the shallot and garlic and cook for 2–3 minutes, until the shallot has softened. Stir in the flour and tomato purée and cook for 1 minute. Stir in the stock, celery, tomatoes and the chopped fresh basil. Season taste with salt and pepper. Cook the mixture over low heat for 20 minutes. Remove from the heat and cool.

2 To make the ravioli, cook the potatoes in a saucepan of boiling water for 10 minutes, until tender. Mash the potatoes in a mixing bowl. Add the egg yolks and oil. Season, then stir in the flour and mix to form a dough.

3 On a lightly floured surface, divide the dough into 24 pieces and shape into flat circles. Spoon the filling onto one half of each circle and fold the dough over to encase the filling, pressing down to seal the edges.

4 Melt the butter in a frying pan and cook the ravioli, in batches, for 6–8 minutes, turning once, until golden. Serve hot, garnished with shredded basil leaves.

potato & spinach gnocchi

ingredients

serves 4

300 g/10½ oz diced floury
   potatoes
175 g/6 oz spinach
1 egg yolk
1 tsp olive oil
125 g/4½ oz plain flour
salt and pepper
spinach leaves, to garnish

sauce

1 tbsp olive oil
2 shallots, chopped
1 garlic clove, crushed
300 ml/10 fl oz passata
2 tsp soft light brown sugar

method

1 Cook the diced potatoes in a saucepan of boiling water
   for 10 minutes, or until cooked through. Drain and
   mash the potatoes.

2 Meanwhile, in a separate saucepan, blanch the spinach
   in a little boiling water for 1–2 minutes. Drain and shred
   the leaves.

3 Transfer the mashed potato to a lightly floured cutting
   board and make a well in the centre. Add the egg yolk,
   olive oil, spinach and a little of the flour. Quickly mix the
   ingredients into the potato, adding more flour as you
   go, to make a smooth, firm dough. Divide the mixture
   into very small dumplings.

4 Cook the gnocchi, in batches, in a saucepan of lightly
   salted, boiling water for about 5 minutes or until they
   rise to the surface.

5 Meanwhile, make the sauce. Put the oil, shallots, garlic,
   passata and sugar into a saucepan and cook over
   low heat for 10–15 minutes or until the sauce has
   thickened and reduced.

6 Drain the gnocchi using a slotted spoon and transfer
   to warm serving dishes. Spoon the sauce over the
   gnocchi and garnish with the fresh spinach leaves.

potato gnocchi with walnut pesto

ingredients

serves 4

450 g/1 lb floury potatoes
55 g/2 oz Parmesan cheese,
    freshly grated
1 egg, beaten
200 g/7 oz plain flour, plus
    extra for dusting
salt and pepper

walnut pesto

40 g/1½ oz fresh flat-leaf parsley
2 tbsp capers, rinsed
2 garlic cloves
175 ml/6 fl oz extra virgin olive oil
70 g/2½ oz walnut halves
40 g/1½ oz pecorino or Parmesan
    cheese, freshly grated

method

1 Boil the potatoes in their skins in a large saucepan of water for 30–35 minutes until tender. Drain well and leave to cool slightly. Meanwhile, to make the walnut pesto, chop the parsley, capers and garlic, then put in a mortar with the oil, walnuts, and salt and pepper to taste. Pound to a coarse paste with a pestle. Add the pecorino cheese and stir well.

2 Peel off the potato skins and pass the flesh through a sieve into a large bowl or press through a potato ricer. While still hot, season well with salt and pepper and add the Parmesan cheese. Beat in the egg and sift in the flour. Lightly mix together, then turn out on to a lightly floured work surface. Knead lightly until the mixture becomes a smooth dough.

3 Roll out the dough on a lightly floured work surface into a long log. Cut into 2.5-cm/1-inch pieces and gently press with a fork to give the traditional ridged effect. Transfer to a floured baking sheet and cover while you make the remaining gnocchi.

4 Bring a large saucepan of water to the boil, add the gnocchi, in small batches, and cook for 1–2 minutes. Remove with a slotted spoon and keep warm while you cook the remaining gnocchi. Serve the gnocchi with a good spoonful of the walnut pesto on top.

baked potatoes with pesto

ingredients

serves 4

4 baking potatoes, about
    225 g/8 oz each
150 ml/5 fl oz double cream
150 ml/5 fl oz vegetable stock
1 tbsp lemon juice
2 garlic cloves, crushed
3 tbsp chopped basil
2 tbsp pine nuts
2 tbsp grated Parmesan cheese
salt and pepper

method

1 Scrub the potatoes well and prick the skins with a fork.
   Rub a little salt into the skins and place on a baking tray.
   Cook in a preheated oven, 190°C/375°F/Gas Mark 5 for
   1 hour, or until the potatoes are cooked through and
   the skins are crisp.

2 Remove the potatoes from the oven and cut them in
   half lengthways. Using a spoon, scoop the potato flesh
   into a mixing bowl, leaving a thin shell of potato inside
   the skins. Mash the potato flesh with a fork.

3 Meanwhile, mix the cream and stock in a saucepan and
   simmer over low heat for about 8–10 minutes, or until
   reduced by half.

4 Stir in the lemon juice, garlic and chopped basil and
   season to taste with salt and pepper. Stir the mixture
   into the mashed potato flesh, together with the
   pine nuts.

5 Spoon the mixture back into the potato shells and
   sprinkle the Parmesan cheese on top. Return to the
   oven for 10 minutes, or until the cheese has browned.
   Serve the potatoes.

stuffed baked potatoes

ingredients

serves 4

900 g/2 lb baking potatoes,
    scrubbed
2 tbsp vegetable oil
1 tsp coarse sea salt
115 g/4 oz butter
1 small onion, chopped
115 g/4 oz grated Cheddar cheese
    or crumbled blue cheese
salt and pepper
snipped fresh chives, to garnish

optional

4 tbsp canned, drained sweetcorn
4 tbsp cooked mushrooms,
    courgette or peppers

method

1 Prick the potatoes in several places with a fork and pu
on a baking sheet. Brush with the oil and sprinkle wit
the salt. Bake in a preheated oven, 190°C/375°F/Gas
Mark 5, for 1 hour, or until the skins are crispy and the
insides are soft when pierced with a fork.

2 Meanwhile, melt 1 tablespoon of the butter in a sma
frying pan over low-medium heat. Add the onion and
cook, stirring occasionally, for 8–10 minutes until soft
and golden. Remove from the heat and set aside.

3 Cut the potatoes in half lengthways. Scoop the flesh
into a large bowl, leaving the skins intact. Set aside
the skins.

4 Coarsely mash the potato flesh and mix in the onion
and remaining butter. Add salt and pepper to taste
and stir in any of the optional ingredients. Spoon the
mixture back into the reserved potato skins. Top with
the cheese.

5 Cook the filled potato skins in the oven for 10 minute
at an increased oven temperature of 200°C/400°F/Ga
Mark 6, or until the cheese has melted and is beginni
to brown. Garnish with chives and serve immediately.

sweetcorn & green bean-filled baked sweet potatoes

ingredients

serves 4

4 red-fleshed sweet potatoes,
about 250 g/9 oz each
115 g/4 oz frozen broad beans
115 g/4 oz frozen sweetcorn
115 g/4 oz fine long green beans
1 tbsp olive oil
1 tbsp balsamic vinegar
140 g/5 oz tomatoes, diced
freshly ground black pepper
2 tbsp torn fresh basil leaves, plus
extra leaves to garnish

method

1 Scrub the sweet potatoes and pierce the skin of each
potato with a sharp knife several times. Arrange on
a baking sheet and bake in a preheated oven, 190°C/
375°F/Gas Mark 5, for 1–1¼ hours or until soft and
tender when pierced with the point of a sharp knife.
Keep warm.

2 When the potatoes are cooked, bring a saucepan of
water to the boil, add the broad beans and sweetcorn
and return to the boil. Reduce the heat, cover and
simmer for 5 minutes. Trim the green beans, cut in
half and add to the saucepan. Return to the boil, then
reduce the heat, cover and simmer for 3 minutes or
until the green beans are just tender.

3 Blend the oil with the vinegar in a small bowl and
season to taste with pepper. Drain the sweetcorn
and beans, return to the pan, add the tomatoes and
pour the dressing over. Add the torn basil leaves and
mix well.

4 Remove the sweet potatoes from the oven, cut in half
lengthways and open up. Divide the sweetcorn and
bean filling between the potatoes and serve at once,
garnished with basil leaves.

sweet potato & mozzarella salad

ingredients

serves 4

2 sweet potatoes, peeled
    and cut into chunks
2 tbsp olive oil
2 garlic cloves, crushed
1 large aubergine, sliced
2 red peppers, deseeded
    and sliced
200 g/7 oz mixed salad leaves
2 x 150 g/5½ oz mozzarella
    cheeses, drained and sliced
pepper
wholewheat bread, to serve

dressing

1 tbsp balsamic vinegar
1 garlic clove, crushed
3 tbsp olive oil
1 small shallot, finely chopped
2 tbsp chopped mixed fresh herbs,
    such as tarragon, chervil
    and basil
pepper

method

1 Put the sweet potato chunks into a roasting tin with
    the oil, pepper to taste and garlic and toss to combine.
    Roast in a preheated oven, 190°C/375°F/Gas Mark 5,
    for 30 minutes, or until soft and slightly charred.

2 Meanwhile, preheat the grill to high. Arrange the
    aubergine and pepper slices on the grill pan and cook
    under the preheated grill, turning occasionally, for
    10 minutes, or until soft and slightly charred.

3 To make the dressing, whisk the balsamic vinegar,
    garlic and oil together in a small bowl and stir in the
    shallot and herbs. Season to taste with pepper.

4 To serve, divide the salad leaves between 4 serving
    plates and arrange the sweet potato, aubergine,
    peppers and mozzarella on top. Drizzle with the
    dressing and serve with wholewheat bread.

potato & cauliflower fritters

ingredients

serves 4

225 g/8 oz diced floury potatoes
225 g/8 oz cauliflower florets
35 g/1¼ oz freshly grated
    Parmesan cheese
1 egg
1 egg white, for coating
vegetable oil, for deep-frying
salt and pepper
paprika, for dusting (optional)
crispy bacon rashers, chopped,
    to serve

method

1 Cook the potatoes in a saucepan of boiling water for about 10 minutes, until cooked through. Drain well and mash with a fork or potato masher.

2 Meanwhile, cook the cauliflower florets in a separate saucepan of boiling water for 10 minutes. Drain thoroughly and gently mix into the mashed potato. Stir in the grated Parmesan cheese and season to taste.

3 Separate the whole egg and beat the yolk into the potato and cauliflower, mixing well. Lightly whisk both the egg whites in a clean bowl, then carefully fold into the potato and cauliflower mixture.

4 Divide the potato mixture into 8 equal portions and shape them into circles. Pour the oil in a frying pan until half full, then heat it until hot. Cook the fritters for 3–5 minutes, turning once halfway through cooking.

5 Dust the fritters with a little paprika, if you like, and serve with the crispy chopped bacon.

chunky potato & spinach curry

ingredients

serves 4

4 tomatoes

2 tbsp groundnut or vegetable oil

2 onions, cut into thick wedges

2.5-cm/1-inch piece fresh ginger,
    peeled and finely chopped

1 garlic clove, chopped

2 tbsp ground coriander

450 g/1 lb potatoes,
    cut into chunks

600 ml/1 pint vegetable stock

1 tbsp Thai red curry paste

225 g/8 oz spinach leaves

method

1 Put the tomatoes in a heatproof bowl and cover with boiling water. Leave for 2–3 minutes, then plunge into cold water and peel off the skins. Cut each tomato into quarters and remove and discard the seeds and central core. Set aside.

2 Heat the oil in a preheated wok, add the onions, ginger and garlic and stir-fry over a medium-high heat for 2–3 minutes until starting to soften. Add the coriander and potatoes and stir-fry for 2–3 minutes. Add the stock and curry paste and bring to the boil, stirring occasionally. Reduce the heat and simmer gently for 10–15 minutes until the potatoes are tender.

3 Add the spinach and the tomato quarters and cook, stirring, for 1 minute, or until the spinach has wilted. Serve immediately

thai potato stir-fry

ingredients

serves 4

900 g/2 lb waxy potatoes,
    cut into small dice
2 tbsp vegetable oil
1 yellow pepper, deseeded
    and diced
1 red pepper, deseeded
    and diced
1 carrot, cut into thin strips
1 courgette, cut into thin strips
2 garlic cloves, crushed
1 red chilli, sliced
1 bunch spring onions,
    halved lengthways
125 ml/4 fl oz coconut milk
1 tsp chopped lemon grass
2 tsp lime juice
finely grated zest of 1 lime
1 tbsp chopped fresh coriander

method

1 Bring a large saucepan of water to the boil and cook
the diced potatoes for 5 minutes. Drain thoroughly.

2 Heat the vegetable oil in a wok or large frying pan,
swirling the oil around the base of the wok until it is
really hot.

3 Add the potatoes, peppers, carrot, courgette, garlic,
and chilli to the wok, and stir-fry the vegetables for
2–3 minutes.

4 Stir in the spring onions, coconut milk, chopped lemo
grass, and lime juice, and stir-fry the mixture for a
further 2 minutes. Add the lime zest and coriander
and stir-fry for 1 minute. Serve hot.

creamy stuffed mushrooms

ingredients

serves 4

25 g/1 oz dried ceps
225 g/8 oz diced floury potatoes
2 tbsp butter, melted
4 tbsp double cream
2 tbsp chopped fresh chives
8 large open-cup mushrooms
25 g/1 oz grated Emmenthal cheese
150 ml/5 fl oz vegetable stock
salt and pepper
fresh chives, to garnish

method

1 Place the dried ceps in a small bowl. Add sufficient boiling water to cover and soak for 20 minutes, then drain and chop finely.

2 Cook the potatoes in a medium saucepan of lightly salted, boiling water for 10 minutes, until cooked through and tender. Drain well and mash until smooth with a fork or potato masher. Mix in the chopped ceps.

3 Blend together the butter, cream and chopped chives and pour into the ceps and potato mixture, mixing well. Season to taste with salt and pepper.

4 Remove the stems from the open-cup mushrooms. Chop the stems and stir them into the potato mixture. Spoon the mixture into the open-cup mushrooms and sprinkle the cheese over the top. Arrange the filled mushrooms in a shallow ovenproof dish and pour in the vegetable stock.

5 Cover the dish and cook in a preheated oven, 220°C/425°F/Gas Mark 7, for 20 minutes. Remove the lid and cook for 5 minutes, until golden. Serve the mushrooms immediately, garnished with the fresh chives.

potato cakes with bacon & maple syrup

ingredients

serves 4

115 g/4 oz cold mashed potatoes
225 ml/8 fl oz milk
75 g/2¾ oz self-raising flour
pinch of salt
1 egg, beaten
corn oil, for cooking

to serve

8 good-quality bacon rashers,
    grilled until crisp
1½ tbsp maple syrup

method

1 Blend the mashed potatoes and milk in a food processor or blender to a thin purée.

2 Sift the flour and salt into a mixing bowl, make a well in the centre of the flour, and add the beaten egg and potato purée. Using a balloon whisk, gradually mix the flour into the liquid ingredients, whisking well to make a smooth, creamy, fairly thick batter.

3 Heat a little oil in a large, non-stick frying pan. Pour a small ladleful of batter per cake into the frying pan – you will probably fit about 3 in the frying pan at one time. Cook each cake for 2 minutes on each side until golden brown. Remove from the frying pan and keep warm while you cook the remaining potato cakes.

4 Divide the cakes between 4 warmed plates, top each serving with 2 bacon rashers, and drizzle with maple syrup.

fishcakes

ingredients

serves 4

450 g/1 lb floury potatoes, peeled and cut into chunks
450 g/1 lb mixed fish fillets, such as cod and salmon, skinned
2 tbsp chopped fresh tarragon
grated rind of 1 lemon
2 tbsp double cream
salt and pepper
1 tbsp plain flour
1 egg, beaten
115 g/4 oz breadcrumbs, made from day-old white or wholewheat bread
4 tbsp vegetable oil, for frying
watercress salad, to serve

method

1 Cook the potatoes in a large saucepan of boiling salted water for 15–20 minutes. Drain thoroughly and mash with a potato masher until smooth.

2 Place the fish in a frying pan and just cover with water. Over a medium heat bring to the boil, then reduce the heat, cover and simmer gently for 5 minutes until cooked. Remove from the heat and drain the fish onto a plate. When cool enough to handle, flake the fish roughly into good-sized pieces, ensuring that there are no bones.

3 Mix the potato with the fish, tarragon, lemon rind and cream. Season well with salt and pepper, then shape into 4 round cakes or 8 smaller ones. Dust the cakes with flour and dip them into the beaten egg. Coat thoroughly in the breadcrumbs. Place on a baking tray and chill for at least 30 minutes.

4 Heat the oil in the frying pan and cook the cakes over medium heat for 5 minutes on each side, turning them carefully using a palette knife or a fish slice.

5 Serve with a crisp watercress salad.

deep-fried fish balls with aïoli

ingredients

serves 4

650 g/1 lb 7 oz floury potatoes,
    roughly chopped
650 g/1 lb 7 oz cod or haddock
    fillets
1 egg yolk, beaten
2 garlic cloves, very finely chopped
2 tbsp chopped fresh parsley
1 tbsp chopped fresh dill
plain flour, for dusting
corn oil, for deep-frying
salt and pepper
fresh watercress or rocket,
    to garnish

aïoli

1 large egg yolk,
    at room temperature
2 large garlic cloves, peeled
salt and pepper
5 tbsp Spanish extra virgin olive oil
5 tbsp corn oil
1 tbsp lemon juice or
    white wine vinegar

method

1 Cook the potatoes in lightly salted boiling water for
20 minutes, until tender. Place the fish in a saucepan,
cover with water, and poach for 8 minutes, or until
flaking.

2 To make the aïoli, whisk together the egg yolk, garlic
and salt until thick. Whisk in a little olive oil, then a little
lemon juice. Continue, adding the oil and lemon juice
alternately, until thick and smooth. Cover and set aside.

3 Transfer the fish to a board. Discard the skin and any
pin bones. Flake the flesh. Drain the potatoes. Mash
with the egg yolk and garlic. Stir in the herbs, then
fold in the fish and season to taste with salt and
pepper. With floured hands, shape into 20 balls.

4 Heat the oil in a large saucepan or deep-fryer to
180–190°C/350–375°F, or until a cube of bread browns
in 30 seconds. Deep-fry the balls, in batches, for
2–3 minutes, or until golden brown. Drain on kitchen
paper. Garnish with watercress or rocket and serve
with the aïoli.

main meals

potato & broccoli pie

ingredients

serves 4

450 g/1 lb waxy potatoes,
    cut into chunks
2 tbsp butter
1 tbsp vegetable oil
175 g/6 oz lean pork, diced
1 red onion, cut into 8 wedges
2½ tbsp plain flour, plus extra
    for dusting
150 ml/5 fl oz vegetable stock
150 ml/5 fl oz milk
75 g/2¾oz dolcelatte
    cheese, crumbled
75 g/2¾oz broccoli florets
25 g/1 oz walnuts
225 g/8 oz ready-made puff
    pastry, thawed if frozen
milk, for glazing
salt and pepper

method

1 Cook the potato chunks in a saucepan of boiling
   water for 5 minutes, then drain and set aside.

2 Meanwhile, heat the butter and oil in a heavy
   saucepan. Add the pork and cook for 5 minutes,
   turning frequently, until browned.

3 Add the onion and cook for 2 minutes more. Stir in
   the flour and cook for 1 minute, then gradually stir
   in the vegetable stock and milk. Bring to the boil,
   stirring constantly.

4 Add the dolcelatte, broccoli florets, potatoes and
   walnuts to the pan and simmer for 5 minutes. Season
   with salt and pepper to taste, then spoon the mixture
   into a pie dish.

5 On a floured work surface, roll out the puff pastry unt
   it is 2.5 cm/1 inch larger than the dish. Cut a 2.5-cm/
   1-inch wide strip from the pastry. Dampen the edge
   of the dish and place the pastry strip around it. Brush
   with milk and put the pastry lid on top.

6 Seal and crimp the edges and make 2 small slits in
   the centre of the lid. Brush with milk and cook in a
   preheated oven, 200°C/400°F/Gas Mark 6, for 25
   minutes, or until the pastry has risen and is golden.

potato, fontina & rosemary tart

ingredients

serves 4

225 g/8 oz ready-made puff
    pastry, thawed if frozen
plain flour, for dusting

filling

3–4 waxy potatoes, peeled
300 g/10½ oz fontina cheese,
    cut into cubes
1 red onion, thinly sliced
3 large fresh rosemary sprigs
2 tbsp olive oil
1 egg yolk
salt and pepper

method

1 Roll out the pastry on a lightly floured work surface
   into a circle about 25 cm/10 inches in diameter and
   put on a baking sheet.

2 Slice the potatoes as thinly as possible so that they
   are almost transparent – use a mandolin if you have
   one. Arrange the potato slices in a spiral, overlapping
   the slices to cover the pastry, leaving a 2-cm/¾-inch
   margin around the edge.

3 Arrange the cheese and onion over the potatoes,
   sprinkle with the rosemary and drizzle over the oil.
   Season to taste with salt and pepper and brush the
   edges with the egg yolk to glaze.

4 Bake in a preheated oven, 190°C/375°F/Gas Mark 5,
   for 25 minutes, or until the potatoes are tender and
   the pastry is brown and crisp. Serve hot.

potato-topped vegetables

ingredients

serves 4

1 carrot, diced
175 g/6 oz cauliflower florets
175 g/6 oz broccoli florets
1 fennel bulb, sliced
75 g/2¾ oz green beans, halved
2 tbsp butter
2½ tbsp plain flour
150 ml/5 fl oz vegetable stock
150 ml/5 fl oz dry white wine
150 ml/5 fl oz milk
175 g/6 oz crimini mushrooms,
    cut into quarters
2 tbsp chopped fresh sage

topping

900 g/2 lb diced floury potatoes
2 tbsp butter
4 tbsp plain yogurt
75 g/2¾ oz freshly grated
    Parmesan cheese
1 tsp fennel seeds
salt and pepper

method

1 Cook the carrot, cauliflower, broccoli, fennel and beans in a large saucepan of boiling water for 10 minutes, until just tender. Drain the vegetables thoroughly and set aside.

2 Melt the butter in a saucepan. Stir in the flour and cook for 1 minute. Remove from the heat and stir in the stock, wine and milk. Return to the heat and bring to the boil, stirring until thickened. Stir in the reserved vegetables, mushrooms and sage.

3 Meanwhile, make the topping. Cook the diced potatoes in a saucepan of boiling water for 10–15 minutes. Drain and mash with the butter, yogurt and half the Parmesan cheese. Stir in the fennel seeds and season to taste.

4 Spoon the vegetable mixture into a 1-litre/1¾ pint pie dish. Spoon the potato over the top and sprinkle with the remaining cheese. Cook in a preheated oven 190°C/375°F/Gas Mark 5, for 30–35 minutes, until the top is golden.

curry pies

ingredients

serves 4

225 g/8 oz plain wholewheat flour
100 g/3½ oz margarine,
    cut into small pieces
4 tbsp water
2 tbsp oil
225 g/8 oz diced root vegetables,
    such as potatoes, carrots
    and parsnips
1 small onion, chopped
2 garlic cloves, finely chopped
½ tsp curry powder
½ tsp ground turmeric
½ tsp ground cumin
½ tsp wholegrain mustard
5 tbsp vegetable stock
soy milk, to glaze

method

1 Place the flour in a mixing bowl and rub in the margarine with your fingertips until the mixture resembles breadcrumbs. Stir in the water and bring together to form a soft dough. Wrap and chill in the refrigerator for 30 minutes.

2 To make the filling, heat the oil in a large saucepan. Add the diced root vegetables, chopped onion and garlic and cook, stirring occasionally, for 2 minutes. Stir in the spices and the mustard, turning the vegetables to coat them thoroughly. Cook the vegetables, stirring constantly, for another minute.

3 Add the stock to the saucepan and bring to the boil. Cover and simmer, stirring occasionally, for about 20 minutes, until the vegetables are tender and the liquid has been absorbed. Set aside to cool.

4 Divide the dough into 4 portions. Roll each portion into a 15-cm/6-inch circle. Place a quarter of the filling in the centre of each circle.

5 Brush the edges of each circle with soy milk, then draw up both sides so that they meet at the top, and pinch the edges firmly together to seal. Place on a baking sheet. Bake in a preheated oven, 200°C/400°F/Gas Mark 6, for 25–30 minutes, until golden brown.

potato, leek & chicken pie

ingredients

serves 4

225 g/8 oz waxy potatoes, diced
5 tbsp butter
1 skinless, boneless chicken
    breast portion, about
    175 g/6 oz, diced
1 leek, sliced
150 g/5½ oz crimini mushrooms,
    sliced
2½ tbsp plain flour
300 ml/10 fl oz milk
1 tbsp Dijon mustard
2 tbsp chopped fresh sage
225 g/8 oz filo pastry, thawed
    if frozen
3 tbsp butter, melted
salt and pepper

method

1 Cook the diced potatoes in a saucepan of boiling water for 5 minutes. Drain and set aside.

2 Melt the butter in a frying pan and cook the chicken for 5 minutes, or until browned all over. Add the leek and mushrooms and cook over medium heat, stirring occasionally, for 3 minutes. Stir in the flour and cook, stirring constantly, for 1 minute. Gradually add the milk and bring to the boil. Add the mustard, chopped sage and potatoes, season and then simmer the mixture for 10 minutes.

3 Meanwhile, line a deep pie dish with half of the sheets of filo pastry. Spoon the sauce into the dish and cover with one sheet of pastry. Brush the pastry with butter and lay another sheet of pastry on top. Brush this sheet with butter.

4 Cut the remaining filo pastry into strips and fold them onto the top of the pie to create an attractive, ruffled effect. Brush the strips with the remaining melted butter and cook the pie in a preheated oven, 180°C/350°F/Gas Mark 4, for 45 minutes, or until golden brown and crisp. Serve hot.

potato, beef & kidney pie

ingredients

serves 4

225 g/8 oz waxy potatoes, diced
2 tbsp butter
450 g/1 lb lean steak, diced
150 g/5½ oz ox kidney,
　cored and chopped
12 shallots
2½ tbsp plain flour, plus extra
　for dusting
150 ml/5 fl oz beef stock
150 ml/5 fl oz light ale
225 g/8 oz ready-made puff
　pastry, thawed if frozen
1 egg, beaten
salt and pepper

method

1 Cook the diced potatoes in a saucepan of boiling wa
　for 10 minutes. Drain thoroughly.

2 Meanwhile, melt the butter in a saucepan and add th
　diced steak and the kidney. Cook over medium heat
　5 minutes, stirring until the meat is sealed on all side
　Add the shallots and cook for 3–4 minutes more. Stir
　the flour and cook for 1 minute. Stir in the beef stock
　and light ale and bring to the boil, stirring constantly

3 Stir the potatoes into the meat mixture and season t
　taste with salt and pepper. Reduce the heat until the
　mixture is just simmering gently. Cover the pan and
　cook for 1 hour, stirring occasionally. Spoon the beef
　mixture into the base of a pie dish.

4 Roll out the pastry on a lightly floured work surface
　to an oval 1-cm/½-inch larger than the top of the dis
　Cut a strip of pastry long enough and wide enough
　fit around the edge of the dish. Brush the edge of the
　dish with beaten egg and press the pastry strip arou
　the edge. Brush with egg and place the pastry lid on
　top. Crimp to seal the edge and then knock up the
　edge of the pastry. Brush with beaten egg to glaze.

5 Cook in a preheated oven, 230°C/450°F/Gas Mark 8
　for 20–25 minutes, or until the pastry has risen and is
　golden brown. Serve immediately.

beef en daube
with mustard mash

ingredients

serves 2

2 tsp vegetable oil
225 g/8 oz extra-lean braising
   steak, cut into 8 pieces
10 small shallots, peeled
   but left whole
1 garlic clove, peeled
   and crushed
1 medium tomato, chopped
225 g/8 oz finely sliced
   mushrooms
150 ml/5 fl oz red wine
100 ml/4 fl oz chicken stock
1 small bouquet garni
1 tsp cornflour
pepper

mustard mash

2 medium floury potatoes,
   peeled and sliced
25 ml/¾ fl oz milk, heated
1 tsp Dijon mustard, to taste

method

1 Heat the oil in a heavy-based flameproof casserole.
   Add the meat and shallots and cook over high heat,
   stirring, for 4–5 minutes to brown the meat on all sides.
   Add the garlic, tomato, mushrooms, wine and stock
   and tuck the bouquet garni well in.

2 Bring to a simmer on the stove, then cover and
   transfer to a preheated oven, 180°C/350°F/Gas Mark 4,
   to cook for 45–60 minutes, or until everything is tender.

3 About 30 minutes before the beef is ready, place
   the potatoes in boiling water and simmer for
   20 minutes, or until just tender. Remove from the heat
   then drain well and put in a bowl. Add the milk and
   mash well. Stir in the mustard to taste and keep warm.

4 Use a slotted spoon to remove the meat and
   vegetables to a warmed serving dish. Cook the
   sauce over high heat until reduced by half. Reduce
   the heat, then remove the bouquet garni and check
   the seasoning.

5 Mix the cornflour with a little cold water to form a
   paste. Add to the sauce, stirring well, and bring back
   to a simmer. Pour the sauce over the meat and serve
   with the mustard mash.

quick baked chicken

ingredients

serves 4

500 g/1 lb 2 oz minced chicken
1 large onion, finely chopped
2 carrots, finely chopped
2 tbsp plain flour
1 tbsp tomato purée
300 ml/10 fl oz chicken stock
pinch of fresh thyme
1.5 kg/3 lb 5 oz mashed potatoes,
    creamed with butter
    and milk and well seasoned
75 g/2¾ oz grated Cheddar cheese
salt and pepper
cooked peas, to serve

method

1 Brown the minced chicken, onion and carrots in a non-stick saucepan for 5 minutes, stirring frequently. Sprinkle the chicken with the flour and cook over low heat for a further 2 minutes.

2 Gradually blend in the tomato purée and chicken stock then simmer for 15 minutes. Season to taste with salt and pepper and add a pinch of fresh thyme. Transfer to a casserole and cool slightly.

3 Spoon the mashed potato over the chicken mixture and sprinkle with cheese. Bake in a preheated oven, 200°C/400°F/Gas Mark 6, for 20 minutes, or until the cheese is bubbling and golden.

4 Serve straight from the casserole, with peas.

variation

For a leaner version, replace the minced chicken with 500 g/1 lb 2 oz minced turkey instead.

potato & turkey pie

ingredients

serves 4

300 g/10½ oz waxy potatoes, diced
2 tbsp butter
1 tbsp vegetable oil
300 g/10½ oz lean turkey meat,
    diced
1 red onion, halved and sliced
2 tbsp plain flour, plus extra
    for dusting
300 ml/10 fl oz milk
150 ml/5 fl oz double cream
2 celery stalks, sliced
75 g/2¾ oz dried apricots, chopped
25 g/1 oz walnut pieces
2 tbsp chopped fresh parsley
225 g/8 oz ready-made
    unsweetened shortcrust pastry,
    thawed if frozen
beaten egg, for brushing
salt and pepper

method

1 Place the diced potatoes in a saucepan of boiling water and cook for 10 minutes, until tender. Drain and set aside.

2 Meanwhile, heat the butter and oil in a heavy saucepan. Add the diced turkey and cook over medium heat, stirring frequently, for 5 minutes, until golden brown.

3 Add the sliced onion and cook for 2–3 minutes. Stir in the flour and cook, stirring constantly, for 1 minute. Gradually stir in the milk and cream. Bring to the boil, stirring, then lower the heat to a simmer.

4 Stir in the celery, apricots, walnut pieces, parsley and potatoes. Season to taste with salt and pepper. Spoon the potato and turkey mixture into the base of a 1.25-litre/2¼-pint pie dish.

5 On a lightly floured work surface, roll out the pastry to 2.5-cm/1-inch larger than the dish. Trim a 2.5-cm/1-inch wide strip and place it on the dampened rim of the dish. Brush with water and cover with the pastry lid

6 Brush the top of the pie with beaten egg to glaze and cook in a preheated oven, 200°C/400°F/Gas Mark 6, for 25–30 minutes, or until the pie is cooked and golden brown. Serve immediately.

fisherman's pie

ingredients

serves 6

110 g/3½ oz butter, plus extra
    for greasing
900 g/2 lb white fish fillets,
    such as plaice, skinned
150 ml/5 fl oz dry white wine
1 tbsp chopped fresh parsley,
    tarragon or dill
175 g/6 oz small mushrooms,
    sliced
175 g/6 oz cooked peeled prawns
40 g/1½ oz plain flour
125 ml/4 fl oz double cream
900 g/2 lb floury potatoes, peeled
    and cut into chunks
salt and pepper

method

1 Fold the fish fillets in half and place in a buttered ovenproof dish. Season well with salt and pepper, pour over the wine and scatter over the herbs. Cover with foil and bake in a preheated oven, 180°C/350°F/Gas Mark 4, for 15 minutes until the fish starts to flake. Strain off the liquid and reserve for the sauce. Increase the oven temperature to 220°C/425°F/Gas Mark 7.

2 Sauté the mushrooms in a frying pan with 15 g/½ oz of the butter and spoon over the fish in the ovenproof dish. Scatter over the prawns.

3 Heat 55 g/2 oz of the butter in a saucepan and stir in the flour. Cook for a few minutes without browning, remove from the heat, then add the reserved cooking liquid gradually, stirring well between each addition. Return to the heat and gently bring to the boil, stirring Add the cream and season to taste with salt and pepper. Pour over the fish and smooth the surface.

4 Meanwhile, cook the potatoes in boiling salted water for 15–20 minutes. Drain well and mash with a potato masher until smooth. Season to taste with salt and pepper and add the remaining butter, stirring until melted. Spoon or pipe the potato onto the fish and sauce and bake for 10–15 minutes until golden brown Serve immediately.

cauliflower & sweet potato curry

ingredients

serves 4

4 tbsp ghee or vegetable oil
2 onions, finely chopped
1 tsp Panch Phoran spice mix
1 cauliflower, broken into
    small florets
350 g/12 oz sweet potatoes, diced
2 fresh green chillies, deseeded
    and finely chopped
1 tsp ginger purée
2 tsp paprika
1½ tsp ground cumin
1 tsp ground turmeric
½ tsp chilli powder
3 tomatoes, quartered
225 g/8 oz fresh or frozen peas
3 tbsp natural yogurt
225 ml/8 fl oz vegetable stock
    or water
salt
1 tsp garam masala
fresh coriander sprigs, to garnish

method

1 Heat the ghee in a large heavy-based frying pan. Add the onions and Panch Phoran and cook over a low heat, stirring frequently, for 10 minutes, or until the onions are golden. Add the cauliflower, sweet potatoes and chillies and cook, stirring frequently, for 3 minutes.

2 Stir in the ginger purée, paprika, cumin, turmeric and chilli powder and cook, stirring constantly, for 3 minutes. Add the tomatoes and peas and stir in the yogurt and stock. Season with salt to taste, cover and simmer for 20 minutes, or until the vegetables are tender.

3 Sprinkle the garam masala over the curry, transfer to a warmed serving dish and serve immediately, garnished with fresh coriander sprigs.

cumin-scented aubergine & potato curry

ingredients

serves 4

1 large aubergine, about
350 g/12 oz
225 g/8 oz potatoes, boiled in their
skins and cooled
3 tbsp sunflower or olive oil
½ tsp black mustard seeds
½ tsp nigella seeds
½ tsp fennel seeds
1 onion, finely chopped
2.5-cm/1-inch piece fresh ginger,
grated
2 fresh green chillies, chopped
(deseeded if you like)
½ tsp ground cumin
1 tsp ground coriander
1 tsp ground turmeric
½ tsp chilli powder
1 tbsp tomato purée
450 ml/15 fl oz warm water
1 tsp salt, or to taste
½ tsp garam masala
2 tbsp chopped fresh coriander
leaves
Indian bread, to serve

method

1 Quarter the aubergine lengthways and cut the stem
end of each quarter into 5-cm/2-inch pieces. Halve th
remaining part of each quarter and cut into the same
size as above. Soak the aubergine pieces in cold wate

2 Peel the potatoes and cut into 5-cm/2-inch cubes.
Heat the oil in a large saucepan over a medium heat.
When hot, add the mustard seeds and, as soon as the
start popping, add the nigella seeds and fennel seeds

3 Add the onion, ginger and chillies and cook for
7–8 minutes, until the mixture begins to brown. Add
the cumin, coriander, turmeric and chilli powder.

4 Cook for about a minute, then add the tomato purée.
Cook for a further minute, pour in the warm water,
then add the salt and aubergine pieces.

5 Bring to the boil and cook over a medium heat for
8–10 minutes, stirring frequently to ensure that the
aubergine cooks evenly. At the start of cooking, the
aubergine will float, but once it soaks up the liquid it
will sink quite quickly. As soon as the aubergine sinks,
add the potatoes and cook for 2–3 minutes, stirring.
Stir in the garam masala and chopped coriander and
remove from the heat. Serve with Indian bread.

sweet potato curry with lentils

ingredients

serves 1

1 tsp vegetable oil

100 g/3½ oz sweet potato, peeled and cut into bite-size cubes

75 g/2¾ oz potato, cut into bite-size cubes

1 small onion, peeled and finely chopped

1 small garlic clove, peeled and finely chopped

1 small fresh green chilli, deseeded and chopped

½ tsp ground ginger

55 g/2 oz dried green lentils

75–100 ml/2½–3½ fl oz hot vegetable stock

pepper

½ tsp garam masala

1 tbsp low-fat plain yogurt

basmati rice, boiled, to serve

method

1 Heat the oil in a non-stick, lidded saucepan and sauté the sweet potato over medium heat, turning occasionally, for 5 minutes.

2 Meanwhile, bring the potato cubes to the boil in a saucepan of water, then simmer until almost cooked (about 6 minutes). Drain and set aside.

3 Remove the sautéed sweet potato cubes with a slotted spoon. Add the onion to the saucepan and cook, stirring occasionally, for 5 minutes, or until transparent. Add the garlic, chilli and ginger and stir for 1 minute.

4 Return the sweet potato to the saucepan with the boiled potato and the lentils, half the stock, pepper to taste and garam masala. Stir to combine, bring to a simmer, and cover. Reduce the heat and simmer gently for 20 minutes, adding a little more stock if the curry looks too dry.

5 Stir in the yogurt and serve with boiled basmati rice.

spanish potatoes

ingredients

serves 4

675 g/1 lb 8 oz diced waxy
    potatoes
3 tbsp olive oil
1 onion, halved and sliced
2 garlic cloves, crushed
400 g/14 oz canned plum
    tomatoes, chopped
75 g/2¾ oz chorizo sausage, sliced
1 green pepper, deseeded and
    cut into strips
½ tsp paprika
25 g/1 oz pitted black olives,
    halved
8 eggs
salt and pepper
1 tbsp chopped fresh parsley
crusty bread, to serve

method

1 Cook the diced potatoes in a saucepan of boiling water for 10 minutes, or until softened. Drain thoroughly and set aside.

2 Heat the olive oil in a large frying pan. Add the sliced onion and garlic and cook gently for 2–3 minutes, until the onion softens.

3 Add the chopped canned tomatoes and cook over low heat for about 10 minutes, until the mixture has reduced slightly.

4 Stir the potatoes into the saucepan with the chorizo, green pepper, paprika and olives. Season to taste with salt and pepper. Cook for 5 minutes, stirring. Transfer to a shallow ovenproof dish.

5 Make 8 small hollows in the top of the mixture with the back of a spoon and carefully break an egg into each hollow. Season the eggs with salt and pepper. Cook in a preheated oven, 220°C/425°F/Gas Mark 7, for 5–6 minutes, or until the eggs are just cooked.

6 Sprinkle the potatoes with chopped parsley and serve immediately with crusty bread.

roasted ratatouille & potato wedges

ingredients

serves 4

300 g/10½ oz potatoes in their skins, scrubbed
200 g/7 oz aubergine, in wedges
125 g/4½ oz red onion, in slices
200 g/7 oz deseeded mixed peppers, in strips
175 g/6 oz courgette, in slices
125 g/4½ oz cherry tomatoes
90 g/3¼ oz fromage frais
1 tsp runny honey
pinch of smoked paprika
1 tsp chopped fresh parsley

marinade

1 tsp vegetable oil
1 tbsp lemon juice
4 tbsp white wine
1 tsp sugar
2 tbsp chopped fresh basil
1 tsp finely chopped fresh rosemary
1 tbsp finely chopped fresh lemon thyme
¼ tsp smoked paprika

method

1 Bake the potatoes in a preheated oven, 200°C/400°F/ Gas Mark 6, for 30 minutes, then remove and cut into wedges – the flesh should not be completely cooked.

2 To make the marinade, place all the ingredients in a bowl and blend with a hand-held electric blender until smooth, or use a food processor.

3 Put the potato wedges into a large bowl with the aubergine, onion, peppers and courgette, then pour over the marinade and mix well.

4 Arrange the vegetables on a non-stick baking tray and roast in the oven, turning occasionally, for 25–30 minutes, or until golden brown and tender. Add the tomatoes for the last 5 minutes of the cooking time just to split the skins and warm slightly.

5 Mix the fromage frais, honey and paprika together in a bowl.

6 Serve the vegetables with the fromage frais mixture, and sprinkled with chopped parsley.

pan haggerty

ingredients

serves 4–5

4 tbsp olive oil
55 g/2 oz butter
450 g/1 lb firm potatoes, Desirée
    or waxy salad potatoes
225 g/8 oz onions, halved and
    thinly sliced
115 g/4 oz Cheddar cheese, grated
salt and pepper

method

1 Heat half the olive oil and half the butter in a 23–25-cm/9–10-inch frying pan.

2 Peel the potatoes if necessary (you don't need to peel small salad potatoes). Slice thinly using a mandolin or food processor. Rinse the slices quickly in cold water and dry thoroughly using a tea towel or kitchen paper. Remove the oil and butter from the heat and arrange the sliced potato in the base of the pan. Build up layers of potato, onion and cheese, seasoning well with salt and pepper between each layer. Finish with a layer of potato and dot the remaining butter over the top.

3 Return to the heat and cook over a medium heat for 15–20 minutes. The base should become brown but not burn. Place a large plate over the frying pan and invert the potato onto the plate by tilting the frying pan. Add the remaining oil to the frying pan and slip the potato back in, cooking the other side for a further 15 minutes until the bottom is crusty. Remove from the heat and serve immediately on a warm plate.

pepper & mushroom hash

ingredients

serves 4

675 g/1lb 8 oz potatoes, diced
1 tbsp olive oil
2 garlic cloves, crushed
1 green pepper, deseeded
    and diced
1 yellow pepper, deseeded
    and diced
3 tomatoes, diced
75 g/2¾ oz button mushrooms,
    halved
1 tbsp Worcestershire sauce
2 tbsp chopped fresh basil
salt and pepper
fresh basil leaves, to garnish

method

1 Cook the diced potatoes in a large saucepan of lightly
   salted boiling water for 7–8 minutes. Drain well
   and reserve.

2 Heat the olive oil in a large heavy-based frying pan.
   Add the potatoes and cook over a medium heat,
   stirring constantly, for about 8–10 minutes, until
   browned. Add the garlic and peppers and cook,
   stirring frequently, for 2–3 minutes.

3 Stir in the tomatoes and mushrooms and cook, stirring
   frequently, for 5–6 minutes.

4 Stir in the Worcestershire sauce and basil and season
   to taste with salt and pepper. Transfer to a warmed
   serving dish and garnish with basil sprigs.

potato & mushroom bake

ingredients

serves 4

2 tbsp butter

500 g/1 lb 2 oz waxy potatoes, thinly sliced and parboiled

150 g/5½ oz sliced mixed mushrooms

1 tbsp chopped fresh rosemary, plus extra to garnish

4 tbsp snipped chives, plus extra to garnish

2 garlic cloves, crushed

150 ml/5 fl oz double cream

salt and pepper

method

1 Grease a shallow, round ovenproof dish with the butter. Layer a quarter of the potatoes in the base of the dish.

2 Arrange one third of the mushrooms on top of the potatoes and sprinkle with one third of the rosemary, chives and garlic. Continue making the layers in the same order, and finish with a layer of potatoes on top.

3 Pour the double cream evenly over the top of the potatoes. Season to taste with salt and pepper. Place the dish in a preheated oven, 190°C/375°F/Gas Mark 5 and cook for about 45 minutes, or until the bake is golden brown and piping hot. Garnish with snipped chives and serve immediately straight from the dish.

potato, herb & smoked salmon gratin

ingredients

serves 6

400 ml/14 fl oz milk
3 whole cloves
2 bay leaves
50 g/1¾ oz onion, sliced
85 g/3 oz leek, chopped
100 g/3½ oz lightly cured smoked salmon, finely sliced into strips
350 g/12 oz potatoes, cut into 2-mm/¹⁄₁₆-inch slices
2 tbsp finely chopped fresh chives
2 tbsp finely chopped fresh dill
1 tbsp finely chopped fresh tarragon
2 tsp wholegrain mustard
pepper
35 g/1¼ oz watercress

method

1 Pour the milk into a large, heavy-based saucepan, add the cloves, bay leaves, onion, leek and smoked salmon and warm over a low heat. When the milk is just about to reach simmering point, carefully remove the smoked salmon with a slotted spoon and cool on a plate.

2 Add the potatoes to the milk and stir with a wooden spoon. Return to a simmer and cook, stirring occasionally to prevent the potatoes from sticking, for 12 minutes, or until the potatoes are just beginning to soften and the milk has thickened slightly from the potato starch. Remove the cloves and bay leaves.

3 Add the herbs, mustard and pepper and stir well. Pour the mixture into a greased and base-lined 19-cm/7½-inch shallow cake tin. Cover with a layer of greaseproof paper and then foil and bake in a preheated oven, 200°C/400°F/Gas Mark 6, for 30 minutes.

4 Remove from the oven and place a pan on top. Cool for 20 minutes before turning out onto a baking sheet. Put under a preheated hot grill to brown the top.

5 Cut the gratin into 6 wedges and serve with the smoked salmon, tossed with watercress.

layered vegetable casserole

ingredients

serves 4

1 tbsp olive oil, for brushing
680 g/1 lb 8 oz potatoes, peeled
    and thinly sliced
2 leeks, trimmed and sliced
2 beef tomatoes, sliced
8 fresh basil leaves
1 garlic clove, finely chopped
150 ml/5 fl oz vegetable stock
salt and pepper

method

1 Brush a large flameproof casserole with a little of the olive oil.

2 Place a layer of potato slices in the bottom of the casserole and cover with a layer of leeks. Top with a layer of tomato slices and a few basil leaves. Repeat these layers until all the vegetables are used up, ending with a layer of potatoes.

3 Stir the garlic into the stock and season to taste with salt and pepper. Pour the stock over the vegetables and brush the top with the remaining oil. Bake in the centre of a preheated oven, 180°C/350°F/Gas Mark 4, for 1½ hours, or until the vegetables are tender and the topping is golden brown. Serve immediately.

french country casserole

ingredients

serves 6

2 tbsp corn oil
2 kg/4 lb 8 oz boneless leg of
    lamb, cut into 2.5-cm/
    1-inch cubes
6 leeks, sliced
1 tbsp plain flour
150 ml/5 fl oz rosé wine
300 ml/10 fl oz chicken stock
1 tbsp tomato purée
1 tbsp sugar
2 tbsp chopped fresh mint
115 g/4 oz dried apricots, chopped
1 kg/2 lb 4 oz potatoes, sliced
3 tbsp melted unsalted butter
salt and pepper
fresh mint sprigs, to garnish

method

1 Heat the oil in a large, flameproof casserole. Cook
   the lamb in batches over medium heat, stirring, for
   5–8 minutes, or until browned. Transfer to a plate.

2 Add the sliced leeks to the casserole and cook, stirring
   occasionally, for 5 minutes, or until softened. Sprinkle
   in the flour and cook, stirring, for 1 minute. Pour in the
   wine and stock and bring to the boil, stirring. Stir in
   the tomato purée, sugar, chopped mint and apricots
   and season to taste.

3 Return the lamb to the casserole and stir. Arrange the
   potato slices on top and brush with the melted butter.
   Cover and bake in a preheated oven, 180°C/350°F/Gas
   Mark 4, for 1½ hours.

4 Increase the oven temperature to 200°C/400°F/Gas
   Mark 6, uncover the casserole and bake for a further
   30 minutes, or until the potato topping is golden
   brown. Serve immediately, garnished with fresh
   mint sprigs.

potato & lemon casserole

ingredients

serves 4

100 ml/3½ fl oz olive oil
2 red onions, cut into 8 wedges
3 garlic cloves, crushed
2 tsp ground cumin
2 tsp ground coriander
pinch of cayenne pepper
1 carrot, thickly sliced
2 small turnips, quartered
1 courgette, sliced
500 g/1 lb 2 oz potatoes,
    thickly sliced
juice and grated rind of 2 large
    lemons
300 ml/10 fl oz vegetable stock
2 tbsp chopped fresh coriander
salt and pepper

method

1 Heat the olive oil in a flameproof casserole. Add the onions and sauté over a medium heat, stirring frequently, for 3 minutes.

2 Add the garlic and cook for 30 seconds. Stir in the ground cumin, ground coriander and cayenne and cook, stirring constantly, for 1 minute. Add the carrot, turnips, courgette and potatoes and stir to coat in the oil.

3 Add the lemon juice and rind and the vegetable stock. Season to taste with salt and pepper. Cover and cook over a medium heat, stirring occasionally, for 20–30 minutes until tender. Remove the lid, sprinkle in the chopped fresh coriander and stir well. Serve immediately.

potatoes in red wine

ingredients

serves 4

125 g/4½ oz butter
450 g/1 lb new potatoes, halved
200 ml/7 fl oz red wine
6 tbsp vegetable stock
8 shallots, halved
125 g/4½ oz oyster mushrooms
1 tbsp chopped fresh sage
    or coriander
salt and pepper
fresh sage leaves or coriander
    sprigs, to garnish

method

1 Melt the butter in a heavy-based frying pan and add the potatoes. Cook over a low heat for 5 minutes, stirring constantly.

2 Add the red wine, vegetable stock and shallots. Season to taste with salt and pepper and simmer for 30 minutes. Stir in the mushrooms and chopped herbs and cook for 5 minutes. Turn the potatoes and mushrooms into a warm serving dish.

3 Garnish with fresh sage leaves and serve immediately.

on the side

perfect roast potatoes

ingredients

serves 6

1.3 kg/3 lb large potatoes,
    such as King Edwards or
    Desirée, peeled and cut into
    even-size chunks
3 tbsp dripping, goose fat,
    duck fat or olive oil
salt

method

1 Cook the potatoes in a large saucepan of lightly salted boiling water over medium heat, covered, for 5–7 minutes. They will still be firm. Remove from the heat. Meanwhile, add the fat to a roasting tin and place in a preheated oven, 220°C/425°F/Gas Mark 7.

2 Drain the potatoes well and return them to the pan. Cover with the lid and firmly shake the pan so that the surface of the potatoes is slightly roughened to help give them a much crisper texture.

3 Remove the roasting tin from the oven and carefully tip the potatoes into the hot fat. Baste them to ensure that they are all coated.

4 Roast the potatoes at the top of the oven for 45–50 minutes, turning the potatoes and basting them once, until they are browned all over and thoroughly crisp.

5 Using a slotted spoon, carefully transfer the potatoes from the roasting tin into a warmed serving dish. Sprinkle with a little salt and serve at once.

chilli roast potatoes

ingredients

serves 4

500 g/1 lb 2 oz small new
      potatoes, scrubbed
150 ml/5 fl oz vegetable oil
1 tsp chilli powder
½ tsp caraway seeds
1 tsp salt
1 tbsp chopped fresh basil

method

1 Cook the potatoes in a saucepan of boiling water for 10 minutes, then drain thoroughly.

2 Pour a little of the oil into a shallow roasting tin to coat the base. Heat the oil in a preheated oven, 200°C/400°F/Gas Mark 6, for 10 minutes. Add the potatoes to the tin and brush them with the hot oil.

3 In a small bowl, combine the chilli powder, caraway seeds and salt. Sprinkle the mixture over the potatoes, turning to coat them all over.

4 Add the remaining oil to the tin and roast in the oven for about 15 minutes, or until the potatoes are cooked through.

5 Using a slotted spoon, remove the potatoes from the oil, draining them thoroughly, and transfer them to a warmed serving dish. Sprinkle the chopped basil over the top and serve immediately.

variation

For an even spicier version, try adding chilli flakes, to taste along with the chilli powder, caraway seeds and salt.

parmesan potatoes

ingredients

serves 4

1.3 kg/3 lb potatoes
salt
50 g/1¾ oz grated Parmesan
    cheese
pinch of freshly grated nutmeg
1 tbsp chopped fresh parsley
vegetable oil, for roasting
4 smoked bacon rashers,
    cut into thin strips

method

1 Cut the potatoes in half lengthways and cook them in a
   saucepan of lightly salted, boiling water for 10 minutes.
   Drain them thoroughly.

2 Combine the grated Parmesan cheese, nutmeg and
   parsley in a shallow bowl. Roll the potato pieces in the
   cheese mixture to coat them completely. Shake off
   any excess.

3 Pour a little oil into a roasting tin and heat it in a
   preheated oven, 200°C/400°F/Gas Mark 6, for
   10 minutes. Remove from the oven and place the
   potatoes in the tin. Return to the oven and cook for
   30 minutes, turning once.

4 Remove from the oven and sprinkle the bacon on top
   of the potatoes. Return to the oven for 15 minutes, or
   until the potatoes and bacon are cooked. Drain off any
   excess fat and serve.

homemade oven chips

ingredients

serves 4

450 g/1 lb large potatoes, peeled
2 tbsp sunflower oil
salt and pepper

method

1 Cut the potatoes into thick, even-sized sticks. Rinse them under cold running water and then dry thoroughly on a clean tea towel. Put in a bowl, add the oil and toss together until coated.

2 Spread the chips on a baking sheet and cook in a preheated oven, 200°C/400°F/Gas Mark 6, for 40–45 minutes, turning once, until golden. Add salt and pepper to taste, and serve hot.

pan-fried potatoes with piquant paprika

ingredients

serves 6

3 tsp paprika

1 tsp ground cumin

¼ – ½ tsp cayenne pepper

½ tsp salt

450 g/1 lb small old potatoes, peeled

corn oil, for pan-frying

sprigs of fresh flat-leaved parsley, to garnish

aïoli, to serve (see below)

aïoli (optional)

1 large egg yolk, at room temperature

2 large garlic cloves, peeled

salt and pepper

5 tbsp Spanish extra virgin olive oil

5 tbsp corn oil

1 tbsp lemon juice or white wine vinegar

method

1 To make the aïoli, whisk together the egg yolk, garlic and salt until thick. Whisk in a little olive oil, then a little lemon juice. Continue, adding the oil and lemon juice alternately, until thick and smooth. Cover and set aside.

2 Put the paprika, cumin, cayenne pepper and salt in a small bowl and mix well together. Set aside.

3 Cut each potato into 8 thick wedges. Pour corn oil into a large, heavy-based frying pan to a depth of about 2.5 cm/1 inch. Heat the oil, then add the potato wedges, preferably in a single layer, and cook gently for 10 minutes, or until golden brown all over, turning from time to time. Remove from the frying pan with a slotted spoon and drain on kitchen paper.

4 Transfer the potato wedges to a large bowl and, while they are still hot, sprinkle with the paprika mixture, then gently toss them together to coat.

5 Turn the potatoes into a large, warmed serving dish and serve hot, garnished with parsley sprigs. Accompany the potatoes with a dipping sauce such as aïoli, if wished.

grilled potatoes with lime mayonnaise

ingredients

serves 4

450 g/1 lb potatoes, unpeeled
    and scrubbed
3 tbsp butter, melted
2 tbsp chopped fresh thyme
salt and pepper
paprika, for dusting

lime mayonnaise

150 ml/5 fl oz mayonnaise
2 tsp lime juice
finely grated rind of 1 lime
1 garlic clove, crushed
pinch of paprika
salt and pepper

method

1 Cut the potatoes into 1-cm/½-inch thick slices. Cook in a saucepan of boiling water for 5–7 minutes; they should still be quite firm. Remove the potatoes with a slotted spoon and drain thoroughly. Line a grill pan with foil, then place the potato slices on the foil.

2 Brush the potatoes with the melted butter and sprinkle the chopped thyme on top. Season to taste with salt and pepper. Cook under a preheated medium grill for 10 minutes, turning them over once.

3 Meanwhile, make the lime mayonnaise. Combine the mayonnaise, lime juice, lime rind, garlic, paprika and salt and pepper to taste in a bowl.

4 Dust the hot potato slices with a little paprika and transfer to a warm serving dish. Serve immediately with the bowl of lime mayonnaise for dipping.

garlic potato wedges

ingredients

serves 4

3 large baking potatoes, scrubbed

4 tbsp olive oil

2 tbsp butter

2 garlic cloves, chopped

1 tbsp chopped fresh rosemary

1 tbsp chopped fresh parsley

1 tbsp chopped fresh thyme

salt and pepper

method

1 Bring a large saucepan of water to the boil. Add the potatoes and parboil them for 10 minutes. Drain the potatoes and refresh under cold water, then drain them again thoroughly.

2 Transfer the potatoes to a cutting board. When the potatoes are cold enough to handle, cut them into thick wedges, but do not peel.

3 Heat the oil and butter in a small saucepan together with the garlic. Cook gently over low heat until the garlic begins to brown, then remove the pan from the heat. Stir in the herbs and season to taste with salt and pepper. Brush the herb mixture all over the potato wedges.

4 Barbecue the potatoes over hot coals or cook under a grill preheated to hot for 10–15 minutes, brushing liberally with any of the remaining herb and butter mixture, until the potato wedges are just tender.

5 Transfer the garlic potato wedges to a warm serving plate to serve.

baby potatoes with aïoli

ingredients

serves 6–8

450 g/1 lb baby new potatoes
1 tbsp chopped fresh
    flat-leaved parsley
salt
aïoli (see page 116)

method

1 To make the aïoli, blend the egg yolk, vinegar, garlic and salt and pepper to taste in a food processor. With the motor still running, very slowly add the olive oil, then the corn oil, drop by drop at first, then, when it starts to thicken, in a slow, steady stream until the sauce is thick and smooth. Alternatively, mix in a bowl with a whisk. Quickly blend in 1 tablespoon water so that the aïoli forms the consistency of sauce.

2 To prepare the potatoes, cut them in half or quarters to make bite-size pieces. If they are very small, you can leave them whole. Put the potatoes in a large saucepan of cold, salted water and bring to the boil. Lower the heat and simmer for 7 minutes, or until just tender. Drain well, then turn out into a large bowl.

3 Transfer the potatoes with aïoli to a warmed serving dish, sprinkle over the parsley and salt to taste. Serve warm with the aïoli as a dip.

herby potatoes & onion

ingredients

serves 4

900 g/2 lb waxy potatoes,
cut into cubes
125 g/4½ oz butter
1 red onion, cut into 8 wedges
2 garlic cloves, crushed
1 tsp lemon juice
2 tbsp chopped fresh thyme
salt and pepper

method

1 Cook the cubed potatoes in a saucepan of boiling salted water for 10 minutes. Drain thoroughly.

2 Melt the butter in a large, heavy-based frying pan and add the red onion wedges, garlic and lemon juice. Cook, stirring constantly for 2–3 minutes.

3 Add the potatoes to the pan and mix well to coat in the butter mixture. Reduce the heat, cover and cook for 25–30 minutes, or until the potatoes are golden brown and tender.

4 Sprinkle the chopped thyme over the top of the potatoes and season to taste with salt and pepper. Transfer to a warm serving dish and serve immediately.

lemony & herbed potatoes

ingredients

serves 8

lemony new potatoes

1 kg/2 lb 4 oz new potatoes
25 g/1 oz butter
1 tbsp finely grated lemon rind
2 tbsp lemon juice
1 tbsp chopped fresh
    dill or chives
salt and pepper
extra chopped fresh dill or chives,
    to garnish

herbed new potatoes

1 kg/2 lb 4 oz new potatoes
3 tbsp light olive oil
1 tbsp white wine vinegar
pinch of dry mustard
pinch of caster sugar
salt and pepper
2 tbsp chopped mixed fresh
    herbs, such as parsley, chives,
    marjoram, basil and rosemary
extra chopped fresh mixed herbs,
    to garnish

method

1 For the lemony potatoes, either scrub the potatoes well or remove the skins by scraping them off with the blade of a sharp knife. Cook the potatoes in plenty of lightly salted, boiling water for about 15 minutes, until just tender. Drain and transfer to a serving bowl.

2 While the potatoes are cooking, melt the butter over low heat. Add the lemon rind, lemon juice and herbs. Season with salt and pepper. Pour the lemony butter mixture over the drained potatoes and stir gently to mix. Garnish with extra herbs and serve hot or warm.

3 For the herbed potatoes, prepare and cook the potatoes as described in step 1. Whisk the olive oil, vinegar, mustard, sugar and seasoning together in a small bowl. Add the chopped herbs and mix well.

4 Pour the oil and vinegar mixture over the drained potatoes, stirring to coat evenly. Garnish with extra fresh herbs and serve warm or cold.

pesto potatoes

ingredients

serves 4

900 g/2 lb small new potatoes
75 g/2¾ oz fresh basil
2 tbsp pine kernels
3 garlic cloves, crushed
100 ml/3½ fl oz olive oil
75 g/2¾ oz mixed Parmesan and
    pecorino cheeses, grated
salt and pepper
fresh basil sprigs, to garnish

method

1 Cook the potatoes in a saucepan of boiling salted water for 15 minutes or until tender. Drain well, transfer to a warm serving dish and keep warm until required.

2 Meanwhile, put the fresh basil, pine kernels, crushed garlic and a little salt and pepper to taste in a food processor. Blend for 30 seconds, adding the oil gradually, until smooth.

3 Remove the mixture from the food processor and transfer it to a mixing bowl. Stir in the grated Parmesan and pecorino cheeses.

4 Spoon the pesto sauce over the potatoes and mix well. Garnish with fresh basil sprigs and serve immediately.

perfect mash

ingredients

serves 4

900 g/2 lb floury potatoes
55 g/2 oz butter
3 tbsp hot milk
salt and pepper

method

1 Peel the potatoes, placing them in cold water as you prepare the others to prevent them from going brown.

2 Cut the potatoes into even-sized chunks and cook in a large saucepan of boiling salted water over a medium heat, covered, for 20–25 minutes, or until they are tender.

3 Remove the pan from the heat and drain the potatoes. Return the potatoes to the hot pan and mash with a potato masher until smooth. Add the butter and continue to mash until it is all mixed in, then add the hot milk.

4 Taste the mash and season with salt and pepper as necessary. Serve at once.

garlic mash

ingredients

serves 4

900 g/2 lb floury potatoes,
    cut into chunks
8 garlic cloves, crushed
150 ml/5 fl oz milk
85 g/3 oz butter
pinch of freshly grated nutmeg
salt and pepper
1 tbsp chopped fresh flat-leaf
    parsley, to garnish

method

1 Put the potatoes in a large saucepan. Add enough cold water to cover and a pinch of salt. Bring to the boil and cook for 10 minutes. Add the garlic and cook for 10 minutes more, until the potatoes are tender.

2 Drain the potatoes and garlic thoroughly, reserving 3 tablespoons of the cooking liquid.

3 Return the reserved liquid to the pan, add the milk and bring to simmering point. Add the butter and return the potatoes and garlic to the pan. Mash thoroughly with a potato masher.

4 Season to taste with nutmeg, salt and pepper and beat the potato mixture with a wooden spoon until light and fluffy. Garnish with flat-leaf parsley and serve immediately.

colcannon

ingredients

serves 4

225 g/8 oz green cabbage,
   shredded
5 tbsp milk
225 g/8 oz floury potatoes, diced
1 large leek, chopped
pinch of freshly grated nutmeg
1 tbsp butter, melted
salt and pepper

method

1 Cook the shredded cabbage in a saucepan of boiling salted water for 7–10 minutes. Drain thoroughly and set aside.

2 Meanwhile, in a separate saucepan, bring the milk to the boil and add the potatoes and leek. Reduce the heat and simmer for 15–20 minutes, or until they are cooked through.

3 Remove from the heat, stir in the freshly grated nutmeg and thoroughly mash the potatoes and leek together. Add the drained cabbage to the mashed potato and leek mixture, season to taste and mix together well.

4 Spoon the mixture into a warmed serving dish, making a hollow in the centre with the back of a spoon. Pour the melted butter into the hollow and serve the colcannon at once, while it is still hot.

potato & cheese gratin

ingredients

serves 4–6

900 g/2 lb waxy potatoes, such
as Charlotte, peeled and
thinly sliced
1 large garlic clove, halved
225 ml/8 fl oz double cream
freshly grated nutmeg
salt and pepper
175 g/6 oz Gruyère cheese,
finely grated
butter, for greasing and dotting
over the top

method

1 Put the potato slices in a bowl, cover with cold
water and set aside for 5 minutes, then drain well.

2 Meanwhile, rub the bottom and sides of an oval
gratin or ovenproof dish with the cut sides of the
garlic halves, pressing down firmly to impart the
flavour. Lightly grease the sides of the dish with butter.

3 Place the potatoes in a bowl with the cream, and
season to taste with freshly grated nutmeg and
salt and pepper. Use your hands to mix everything
together, then transfer the potatoes to the gratin dish
and pour over any cream remaining in the bowl.

4 Sprinkle the cheese over the top and dot with butter.
Place the gratin dish on a baking sheet and bake in a
preheated oven, 190°C/375°F/Gas Mark 5, for 60–80
minutes, or until the potatoes are tender when pierced
with a skewer and the top is golden and bubbling. Let
it stand for about 2 minutes, then serve straight from
the gratin dish.

pommes anna

ingredients

serves 4

675 g/1 lb 8 oz waxy potatoes
5 tbsp butter, melted
4 tbsp chopped mixed herbs
salt and pepper
chopped fresh herbs, to garnish

method

1 Slice the potatoes thinly and pat dry with kitchen paper. Arrange a layer of potato slices in a lightly greased shallow ovenproof dish until the base is covered. Brush with a little butter and sprinkle with a quarter of the chopped mixed herbs. Season to taste.

2 Continue layering the potato slices, brushing each layer with melted butter and sprinkling with herbs, until they are all used up.

3 Brush the top layer of potato slices with butter. Cover the dish and cook in a preheated oven, 190°C/375°F/ Gas Mark 5, for 1½ hours.

4 Turn out onto a warm ovenproof platter and return to the oven for 25–30 minutes more, until golden brown. Serve, garnished with the chopped herbs.

potatoes à la boulangère

ingredients

serves 2

400 g/14 oz potatoes, very
   thinly sliced
1 small onion, peeled and
   thinly sliced
freshly ground black pepper,
   to taste
55 ml/2 fl oz vegetable stock
55 ml/2 fl oz skimmed milk
1 tsp butter

method

1 Layer the potato and onion slices in a shallow,
   ovenproof dish, seasoning each layer well with pepper.

2 Mix the stock and milk together and pour over the
   potatoes. Dot the top layer with the butter, then cover
   with foil and bake in a preheated oven, 190°C/375°F/
   Gas Mark 5, for 30 minutes.

3 Remove the foil and cook for a further 30 minutes,
   or until the potatoes are cooked.

garlic & chilli-flavoured potatoes with cauliflower

ingredients

serves 4

350 g/12 oz new potatoes, peeled if preferred
1 small cauliflower
2 tbsp sunflower or olive oil
1 tsp black or brown mustard seeds
1 tsp cumin seeds
5 large garlic cloves, lightly crushed, then chopped
1–2 green chillies, finely chopped (deseeded if you like)
½ tsp ground turmeric
½ tsp salt, or to taste
2 tbsp chopped fresh coriander leaves

method

1 Cook the potatoes in their skins in a saucepan of boiling water for 20 minutes, or until tender. Drain, then soak in cold water for 30 minutes. Halve or quarter the potatoes according to their size – they should be only slightly bigger than the cauliflower florets.

2 Meanwhile, divide the cauliflower into about 1-cm/½-inch diameter florets and blanch in a large saucepan of boiling salted water for 3 minutes. Drain and plunge into iced water to prevent further cooking, then drain again.

3 Heat the oil in a medium-sized saucepan over a medium heat. When hot, add the mustard seeds, then the cumin seeds. Remove from the heat and add the garlic and chillies. Return to a low heat and cook, stirring, until the garlic has a light brown tinge.

4 Stir in the turmeric, followed by the cauliflower and the potatoes. Add the salt, increase the heat slightly and cook, stirring, until the vegetables are well blended with the spices and heated through.

5 Stir in the coriander, remove from the heat and serve immediately to accompany any Indian main course dish.

bombay potatoes

ingredients

serves 4

1 kg/2 lb 4 oz waxy potatoes
2 tbsp vegetable ghee
1 tsp Panch Poran spice mix
3 tsp ground turmeric
2 tbsp tomato purée
300 ml/10 fl oz plain yogurt
salt
chopped fresh coriander,
    to garnish

method

1 Put the whole potatoes into a large saucepan of salted cold water. Bring to the boil, then simmer for about 15 minutes, until the potatoes are just cooked, but not tender.

2 Heat the ghee in a separate saucepan over medium heat and add the Panch Poran, turmeric, tomato purée, yogurt and salt. Bring to the boil and simmer, uncovered, for 5 minutes.

3 Drain the potatoes and cut each one into 4 pieces. Add the potatoes to the pan, then cover, and cook briefly. Transfer to an ovenproof casserole. Cook in a preheated oven, 180°C/350°F/Gas Mark 4, for about 40 minutes, or until the potatoes are tender and the sauce has thickened a little.

4 Sprinkle with chopped coriander to garnish and serve the Bombay potatoes immediately.

curried potato, cauliflower & spinach

ingredients

serves 4

2 tbsp olive oil
1 onion, diced
1 tbsp garam masala
½ tsp ground cumin
1 tsp ground turmeric
400 g/14 oz canned chopped
    tomatoes in tomato juice
300 ml/10 fl oz vegetable stock
450 g/1 lb new potatoes,
    cut into chunks
280 g/10 oz cauliflower florets
55 g/2 oz flaked almonds
250 g/9 oz baby spinach leaves
naan bread, to serve

method

1 Heat the oil in a saucepan over low-medium heat, add the onion and spices and cook, stirring constantly, for 2–3 minutes, taking care not to burn the spices. Add the tomatoes and stock and bring to the boil, then reduce the heat, cover and simmer for 25 minutes.

2 Meanwhile, put the potatoes into a separate saucepan, cover with cold water, and bring to the boil. Reduce the heat, cover and simmer for 15 minutes. Add the cauliflower and return to the boil, then reduce the heat, cover and simmer for a further 10 minutes, or until just tender.

3 Meanwhile, preheat the grill to medium. Spread the almonds out in a single layer on a baking sheet and toast under the grill, turning to brown evenly, for 1–2 minutes – watch constantly because they brown very quickly. Tip into a small dish and set aside.

4 Add the spinach to the potatoes and cauliflower, stir into the water and simmer for 1 minute. Drain the vegetables and return to the pan. Stir in the curried tomato sauce. Transfer to a warmed serving dish, sprinkle over the toasted almonds and serve at once with naan bread.

index